My Struggle

14622-THEC

My Struggle

The Chicks Suck Guy

This book is dedicated to Amy, the first chick who saw my qualities and decided that she liked them. Not only that, but after almost three years she still actually likes me for me. She has also let me explore her anally, and that truly makes her special.

Introduction Part One:

Self-Publishing Blows

It has come down to this. I have an extremely popular Web page and I announce that I'm writing a book and that I'm looking for a publisher or an agent and not one of you helps me. How many millions of page views have I generated? How many of you losers have I educated? And not one of you could help me get published, so I have to reformat my entire manuscript and put up my own money so I can get this book into your hands.

That's my way of saying, "Thanks for buying this book." I'm not looking to get rich off of this thing; I just want to get this book out of my life. There are so many other things I'd rather be doing. Since you're reading this, chances are that you've been a fan of mine for quite a while and I really thank you for buying this book as that gives me more money to spend on porn.

What sucks about this whole self-publishing thing is that the covers of most of these books really suck. They all look generic and stupid. I'm not even going to see the cover of my own book until it's printed. Just retarded, I tell you.

But self-publishing may be good for me. I think only losers self-publish, because they don't have the talent or dedication to do things the right way. When it comes to dating, I'm a loser. So maybe it fits. But I still hate self-publishing.

I will say, though, that the people at Xlibris have completely exceeded my expectations in every way, and I'm not just saying that so they'll finish my book quicker. Really, they have made this book better than it was when it was just a manuscript.

What follows is the original introduction to this book. I wrote it assuming that a book deal would just fall into my crotch. I apparently made that assumption about women too. Publishing a book is just as hard as trying to fuck that broad that won't talk to you.

One final note: portions of this book are written in stream-of-consciousness style. I apologize for that, but that style is the best way for you to get inside my head because you certainly aren't getting inside any other parts of my body.

Introduction Part Two:

Welcome to My Personal Hell

When I started my Web site in February 1998, I had no idea how popular the page would become. The following paragraphs were on the main page:

I am almost any woman's dream come true. I am smart, funny, totally honest, easy to talk to, and easy to get along with. I could never ever ever cheat on my chick. I would have such a guilty conscience that if I did, I would wind up killing myself. I couldn't even lie to my chick. And even though I am not rich, it's obvious to anyone with half a brain that I will be successful at whatever I choose to do. In other words, I will someday have lots of money. I am 20 years old, and make more than most 20 year olds in my region of the country, working at a job that I earned myself.

I can't get laid.

That's not entirely true, so maybe I should rephrase that.

I can't find a good chick.

Hmm. That's not entirely true either. So, here's my real problem:

I can't find a good chick who will even go out with me!

What do I mean by a "good chick?" Why spend time on a website when I could instead be looking for a "good chick?" Am I a wuss, or am I completely normal?

These questions, and more, is what this site is devoted to.

When you read my rants and stories, keep the above passage in mind. This book is not a "women-bashing" book, nor is it a "guys are superior to girls" book. This book, like the site, is the text version of me. I didn't start the site hoping to get 100,000 hits. I didn't start the site to amuse people and make them laugh and think at the same time. I didn't even start the site to get chicks to send topless pictures of themselves to me, although all of the above are nice benefits.

So, why *did* I start the site? The answer is simple. I wanted to make money off a book deal.

Seriously, I wanted to see if anyone could tell me what was wrong with me. Maybe someone could tell me why I have all these good qualities, but can't get a date.

What I discovered was that I wasn't alone. I've gotten seemingly thousands of emails from guys that say, "I'm just like you," or "I used to be just like you." I would like to think that everyone loves this site because of my own little quirks and anecdotes, but that's not the case. The reason I think the site is so popular is that so many people, of both sexes, can identify with it.

For a long time, I was completely baffled by Chicks Suck's popularity. After the site got really popular, I noticed that whenever a group of people got together, dating was a big discussion topic and that *everybody hates today's dating scene.*

What you are about to read, should you choose to read it, is what I believe is The Truth. I have women figured out. Feminism, the media, bad parenting, and idiocy have all made the females in the United States complete morons. Either females:

    a)   Hold out for Prince Charming

    b)   Reject what they're supposed to want and go for the loser guys

    c)   Both a) and b)

What women have failed to realize is that there is no Prince Charming, and going out with loser guys to piss off Daddy and add drama to their miserable lives will only hurt themselves in the long run. So, these chicks complain about how they can't find a good guy to their best male friends. Meanwhile, their male friends would kill newborn babies just for a chance at the woman of their dreams.

What women **say they want** and **who they fuck** are two separate things. I am exactly what women *say* they want, and I can't even get a date. If Amy left me tomorrow, it would probably be years before I even have another date.

I've been told that what's wrong with me is that I am a nice guy. I believe that, but I've seen nice guys get chicks too. There has got to be something more. Maybe I am wrong for thinking that. Why should I want a more complicated explanation of what's wrong with me?

There is no doubt in my mind, that someday, somewhere, I will meet the girl of my dreams, the woman who was made just for me. She'll have a great sense of humor, a great personality, intelligence, and maybe even a great body.

And she'll also have a boyfriend.

I hope you enjoy the book.

The Chicks Suck Guy
http://www.chickssuck.com

CHAPTER 1

The Rules

Like my Web site, many people will see the title of this book and will not bother to open it up, because they are offended. On the other hand, some people will read into all of my stories and rants and try to come up with their own conclusions, so I felt that this had to be the very first chapter.

The word "chick" was never meant to demean or offend anyone, yet people are offended by the term. The word "chick" isn't like the word "nigger." There's no power behind the word "chick," and if I were black, I'd be offended that someone had made a comparison like that.

Can you imagine someone using the word "chick" like they use the word "nigger?" It's almost laughable!

"A bunch of chicks are moving into the neighborhood! We better start looking for a new place to live."

"So I was walking down the street, and some chicks were behind me, and they started following me! I got scared and walked as fast as I could to my car."

"Yo yo! What's up my chickz! In da houuuuuse!" (To be used only if you're a chick talking to other chicks.)

"Fucking chick!"

As you can see, the word "chick" has nowhere near the power of other racial slurs such as "nigger," "kike," "spic," "dago," "chink," "slopehead," "porch monkey," "cracka," "mic," "fish eater," "dot face," "vine swinger," "wop," "towel head," "berry picker," "Michelli," "Narrow Back," "Piffke," "Roo," "Caucasianally-challenged," "Windchimes," "Snow Nigger," "Point-Six," "Pork and Cheese," "Buckethead," "Lemonhead," "Lincoln's Mistake," "Moosefucker," "Petrol Sniffer," "Ric," "Tabeetsu," "Tater tot," or "dirty fucking Jew."[1]

I'm not anti-chick. I love chicks. I don't refer to them in general as bitches or whores, but every once in a while I admit to slipping and calling them cunts. Hey, nobody's above being called a cunt. Not even you.

I'm not anti-chick, but I *am* against their behavior. For 23 years, I have heard, "There are no decent men! All men are scum!"

All most chicks do is complain about guys. Guys aren't perfect by any means, but I've discovered that there are many guys out there who want more than just a good lay.

That, and I hear chicks use the word "chick" every day! This isn't a case like "nigger," where the word is so demeaning that it isn't even included in Microsoft Word 97's spell checking dictionary (for the record, Microsoft did put the word into their Office 2000 suite). Chicks use the term to describe other chicks, so why can't I?

Also, there is no difference at all between a woman and a chick, not in my book anyway (and you're reading *my* book). People have emailed me and said, "Your problem is that you're going after chicks. You need a *woman!*"

Give me a break! Ninety percent of all chicks are identical in their behavior up until the age of 45. They can't make up their minds about anything at all, and that includes things that ordinary people don't have problems with. Guys know what they want for dinner, what they want out of their lives, and what they want in a mate.

Most chicks don't seriously begin thinking about any of that stuff until around the age of 25, and some don't begin until after they're 30 or higher. Once they realize that a tall, dark, handsome man isn't going to come and sweep them off their feet, they face the fact that they will soon be considered an old hag if they don't marry.

So, around the age of 45, they start to come to their senses. Unfortunately, by then, they look like 45 year olds. And they're only a few years away from menopause, where they become mega-bitches and have hot flashes and such, so they aren't worth the trouble.

---

[1] Check out the Racial Slur Database (http://rsdb.fuck.org/) to find out the meanings of terms you do not know.

As this book is semi-autobiographical, you're going to think that the stories I'm giving are somewhat skewed, or that the things I say in my rants are not the exact things I say in real life. All my stories are skewed somewhat; they have to be, as they come from my perceptions. I've tried to give an unbiased, completely impartial view of life situations that I describe. But I obviously can't give the whole story. Not unless I go up to one of the chicks I've talked about and say, "Yeah, I'm writing a book, and you're part of it. Would you mind telling me if you agree with me when I call you a fucking psycho-cunt who screws with others' minds just so she can feel good about herself?"

I get email saying things like, "No wonder you can't get a date! If you talked like that around me, I would never consider you."

Everyone has a different voice in their head when they read. Along with that, some people have only their perspective, and they can't even *understand* why someone who disagrees with them could possibly do so.

Sometimes I talk to chicks just like I do in my rants. Sometimes it'll even be a whole class, or a comedy club filled with strangers. And everyone wholeheartedly agrees with what I say.

To people who know me really well, yes, I am very much like the person on my site. That's why I describe it as the text version of me. My site is simple, honest, not particularly easy on the eyes but still okay to look at, and also in 12-point font, just like me.

As for how I come across? If anything, I come across much nicer in real life. Once you know me, I'm the same as on my site, but I'm still generally a polite, soft-spoken individual. Unless I disagree with you. Then I'm a loud-mouthed son of a bitch.

While reading this book, or surfing my site, please don't make suppositions. Only go by what I tell you. There's nothing more bothersome than a person who means well, trying to give me advice, saying, "Here's what your problem is," and then they proceed to tell me that I keep going on and on about how great I am, and that if I stopped doing that, I'd probably get a chick.

Or the fact that I spend so much time making a web site means that I'm neurotic.

Or that I will become a stalker, it's just a matter of time.

Or that I think racial jokes are funny means I'm some sort of KKK-wannabe with only two teeth. (For the record, I have six teeth.)

All of the above is incorrect. I don't always talk about how great I am, but I have to on the site, because if I didn't talk about me, what the hell would I talk about? I am not God's gift to chicks, but I'm not a wuss who can't approach chicks either. All I have ever claimed to be is decent boyfriend material. No more, no less. The Web site takes hardly any of my time, and I have never shown any patterns of being a stalker. If I were a stalker, I'd still be chasing every chick mentioned on my site. And I'd be getting some!

And believe me, people can laugh at racial jokes and not be racist. Just like someone can laugh at a Monica Lewinsky joke without ever sticking a cigar up a chick's pussy, or having one stuck up theirs[2].

Finally, I do not whine. I bitch. I moan. I complain. I dream. I hope. But I do not whine. Chicks whine. I merely point out how society should change to make all of our social lives better.

So, those are the rules. If you don't abide by them, then you will not get the point of this book, and I advise you to put this book down right now and do society a favor and kill yourself. Before you do, please take the rest of your money and buy more copies of this book. If enough of these sell, I'll never have to write another book again, and in your mind, you'll be doing society a favor by helping to silence me.

Overdosing on sleeping pills is probably the simplest and least painful way to kill yourself. And if you can't even get that right, you're a bigger loser than I am.

---

[2] Microsoft Word wanted to change the word "theirs" to "his or hers." The sentence is much funnier with Microsoft's suggestion.

CHAPTER 2

My First True Love

Most people speak highly of their first true love. At least that's the stereotype. Some people even marry their first true love. I wish I could have had that simplicity. Imagine, finding the girl of your dreams when you're 9, 13, or 15 years old and realizing that's the person you want to spend the rest of your life with. I imagine it's a magical feeling. I even think I had the feeling.

Then again, I probably didn't.

I am extremely white, thus I sunburn really easily. I remember going swimming when I was a kid. I once swam for 15 minutes and came home sunburned. I eventually started to dislike swimming, and I guess even before then, decided that being indoors with air conditioning was preferable to being outside in the hot sun.[3]

I watched a lot of television. More than the average kid did, that was for sure. I think in third grade I had figured out that I watched between eight to ten hours a day. I was a pretty bright kid, so homework was never a problem for me, even in high school. My Atari 800 computer got really old after 1986, and I didn't get a Nintendo Entertainment System until the last days of 1988. (I am still bitter about that, damned cheapskate parents.) So, for quite a bit of my young life, television was what I did. I sure didn't talk to my parents or my sister, and if I did, it was to tell them I really wanted a Nintendo.

When I say I watched a lot of TV, don't make the mistake of thinking I was a discriminating viewer. Oh no, I watched everything. I can't believe the crap I watched. I remember being 8 or 9 years old

---

[3] I lived in Texas. The sun felt really hot there. Probably still does.

and actually being disappointed that *Full House* had been preempted! I'd watch every sitcom, from *Who's the Boss,* the whitest sitcom there was, to *Amen* and *227,* two sitcoms by blacks for blacks. I was pissed off during the summer of the Oliver North trial, because all of the game shows like *Price Is Right, Press Your Luck,* and *Scrabble* were not on the air. Fucking Iran Contra Arms For Hostages deal. I don't care if Americans would have died! I just want to see who wins on *Hot Potato.*

Nintendo helped get me away from some of that, but I still watched. You can only sit in front of a television with a game controller for so long before you get sick of it. Of course, when I got sick of it, I'd just sit in front of the television without a game controller and watch *Growing Pains, Head of the Class,* or *Mr. Belvedere.* (That Wesley was such a troublemaker!)

These sitcoms all eventually did a show where a male character and a female character would like each other, and neither one knew it, and in the end, they would get together and all was good. You know, I knew real life didn't have a laugh track just like I knew that *The Cosbys* were the whitest black family in America. I didn't believe anything on these sitcoms, but when it came to matters of the heart, I was extremely naïve. I had never even seen my parents kiss, but I saw parents kissing weekly on *Alf.* I guess I knew my family was different. So when I did find a girl for whom I would fall, it would all work out.

That's the only way I can explain my naiveté. I honestly believed that in love, people would really be honest with each other and it would all magically work out. How else could I have been so dumb? Perhaps I'm just extremely idealistic when it comes to this stuff in the first place.

* * *

I had lived in this city for one and a half years. I had gone to my high school since the middle of my tenth-grade year. I never saw her until my senior year, almost a year and a half since I started going to this school. When I first saw her, I don't think that I thought much of her. I was probably wrapped up in too many other things to notice. I was prepared to get out of high school, really. I was getting sick of that place.

The one class I had with her, indeed the only class I ever had with her in high school, was very loosely structured. When there was nothing to do, there was literally nothing to do except talk and hang out. It was kind of cool. And the fact that the whole class was made up of nothing but seniors who didn't give a shit, well, we were pretty damned free.

The first time I ever really noticed her was homecoming that year. She wore this sparkling blue dress that looked like it had come straight from Japan. The dress was exotic, and most exotic things have a tendency of looking very different. I went up to her and told her I loved the dress and she looked great in it. I really meant that. That was not a comment to get down her pants or anything else. I was just stunned by her beauty.

I started talking to her daily, sitting next to her in class, and we talked like we had known each other for ages. I never felt nervous around her nor did I feel self-conscious. I even started to realize that I wanted to be more than friends. I had never felt any of these feelings for anybody before.

About a week before Christmas Break, she and I were alone, and she said, "You're just like my boyfriend. You guys would like each other a lot."

Why don't you just take a fucking knife and stab it through my heart and twist it around and around and around? Or take a hammer to my nuts. I was just devastated. I really was crushed.

Then we went on Christmas Break, which was about a week and a half. What the fuck was up with Christmas Break? I remember being in kindergarten and having three weeks off. It's like every year they take three days off the thing. It actually got to the point one year that I was in class on December 23! Ugh.

So, anyway, I was on Christmas Break, and I could not stop thinking about her. I fucking missed her! Shit! Every day I would think about seeing her again. I probably even dreamed about her. And over and over again, I could hear her saying, "You're just like my boyfriend."

Well, goddammit! If I'm just like your boyfriend then it shouldn't be hard for me to replace him, then, should it?

I did some asking around and I found out who her boyfriend was.

It was some guy who graduated in the last class. I didn't know him at all, but I did know he wasn't going to college or anything. I don't know what he did, actually, but I knew he was not in school. Pretty odd, I thought. But of course, I was college bound, and so was she. Me 1, boyfriend 0. (Boy, was I naïve.)

A few days after we got back from our three-day Christmas Break, I was sitting next to her in class. Our teacher said, "Hey, are you guys going to go to Prom as a couple? You guys would make a great couple, you know."

Oh thank you thank you thank you, dude! You just gave me an opening.

"Oh, I know. Wouldn't we? I bet you we will go as a couple." I then turned and winked at her. Her response?

"Ohmigod ohmigod ohmigod!"

Well, hey, my feelings were at least public and that was only my first step to defeating her faceless bum of a boyfriend.

I also called her a few times, and every time I did we stayed on the phone for *hours*. We had long, fulfilling conversations. I liked her even more, knowing that I could talk to her for vast periods of time. One night, my cat was in my room while I was talking to her. She was lying down next to the door. I was on the phone with her for almost two hours, and as soon as I hung up the phone, my cat meowed to get out. It was instantaneous. My cat realized my enthusiasm and did not want to interrupt me. Wow.

Not only did I have great conversations with her, but I also got her to join some after-school club with me. Yes! More time with her! Woo hoo!

So I worked with her in this club, and eventually we had to go out of town. We went out of town on a Saturday. Friday, she was okay with me. Saturday, something was wrong. She was being extremely rude to me and gave me one of the coldest shoulders I've ever been given by anyone. I had no clue what the hell was up. Maybe it was her time of the month. Hey, I'm a considerate guy. I could respect that.

The day before that Saturday, there was some message exchange program or something that the school was doing. I figured it'd be neat to send her one. It basically said something like if I ever got to kiss

her, I'd be so nervous that I'd probably vomit down her throat, and
that would make her barf herself, and we'd be throwing up together
and that would be really romantic. Really stupid and juvenile. I gave
it to the messenger on Friday. He would deliver it Monday, maybe. It
just so happened that the messenger really hated me, so when Monday came around and she didn't say anything about it then, or on
Tuesday, or Wednesday, I just figured she'd never gotten it.

I'm sure most of you have figured out why she was mad at me, and
if you haven't by now, you're a real dumbass. I never put the two
things together because I honestly did it as a joke, and besides, she
never got the thing, otherwise she would have told me. (Try to hold
back your laughter.)

That was in the beginning of March.

Fast forward to the middle of April. Things are actually okay between her and me, and while I was driving us to our after-school extra-curricular activity, I noticed her boyfriend was following us. Now,
I wasn't in the car with her by myself, so he had no reason to be
pissed at me. When we got to our destination, she got out and talked
to him, then came over to me and said, "Look, I've really got to go. I'm
sorry."

"OK," I said.

She left. During that meeting, there was a permission slip that had
to be signed and returned the next day. Well, how was she going to
sign and return it if she never got it? I'll just stop by her place on my
way home . . .

I pulled up into her driveway, got out of my car, and knocked on
her door. No answer. Hmph. That's odd. I knew she was home. I heard
some voices from inside. Knocked again. Guess who answered the door.

HIM. My archrival. The one who was depriving me of what would
make me happy. HIM. I didn't miss a beat, though.

"Hey man, can you give this to her for me? She has to get it
signed and returned tomorrow or she can't go on the trip," I said.

"Yeah, sure. Look dude, I don't appreciate you hitting on my girlfriend and writing her notes."

There was a short pause.

"Uh, what are you talking about?" I asked, puzzled.

"I'm talking about *this*," he held up the note that I had written in March, about a month earlier.

I was shocked.

"Look man, I didn't know she ever got that. I wrote it as a complete joke and the messenger I gave it to hated me. She never said a word about it to me, so I never even knew she got it. If she had confronted me, I would have explained that. Sorry. It was just a joke."

"Oh, okay."

"Later man," I said.

I had no idea of it at the time, but this was my first exposure to how crazy most chicks really are.

As I walked seven or eight paces back to my car, I couldn't believe what was going on. They were fighting, and they were fighting over me. Holy shit! She will be mine, oh yes, she will be mine. I am one reason they are having problems in their relationship. Here he is, following her after she gets off of school, and here I am just saying, "Do what you want." Wow. This is great. Plus, there are two weeks until Prom. I hadn't planned on going, but shit, I'd go with her! Wow. I just better pretend to look disappointed when I hear that they've broken up.

I must say, though, that while I was courting her, it must have been very tough on her. The people I hung out with knew of my feelings for her, and they would bring me up to her almost every time they saw her. I would have told them to stop it if I had known any better, but really, it must have seemed to her like I was a cloud from which she just could not escape. Every day someone was mentioning my name, bringing me up to her. I was enveloping her, in an indirect way.

She didn't come to school the next two days. Oh, this was great! They had definitely broken up. When she did come back, I heard that they really had broken up, although not from her. Who the fuck cared why, they weren't a couple anymore and I could finally make my move and live happily ever after.

Right in front of me, someone else asked her if she was going to Prom. She said no. I tried to keep things positive. She had been going out with this goober for almost a year; she probably ain't going to rebound quickly.

And actually, I put this chick on a pedestal. I have not fallen harder for anyone else since her, and hopefully never will again. She was a goddess to me, and she could do no wrong.

Undaunted, I brought her a few graduation gifts. I didn't have a lot of money, but I spent the little I had on her, hoping she would appreciate it. I got a hug from her, and that was all I needed. I was really happy just getting a hug.

What graduation gift did she give me? It's funny how memory can fade. Let me think, what was it she got me? Hmm . . . oh yeah! I remember!

NOTHING.

Of course, she was a goddess so that was okay with me. My love was unconditional.

She played violin, and I found out she was having a recital from one of her friends. Funny, she never told me about her senior recital. Wouldn't it be perfect if I just showed up by myself out of nowhere? Wouldn't that be a nice thing to do?

So I did. I heard her play and afterwards there was a reception. I told her I thought she did a good job and her mom came over and struck up a conversation with me. Her mom really liked me. Really, really liked me, I could tell. I got this vibe from her that she knew I was the better man for her daughter. Her mom knew my name without me even telling her, and she was always warm and friendly towards me. I really liked the fact that I was being talked about, obviously in a positive way if her mom liked me. And if I'm wrong about everything else in this book (and I'm not), the one thing I know I'm right about is how much her mom liked me. I only met her mom twice, though. I thought her mom liking me was a good thing, but looking back, I believe that it was just another nail in the coffin. And of course, I showed up at her recital, and HE didn't.

We (she and I, not her mom) were going to attend the same college and even wound up having a class together. But I'm getting ahead of myself, really. Do you know how many times she called me over the summer? Let me count . . . this may take a while . . .

NONE.

I had failed. For the first time in my life, I had failed at something that meant a lot to me. It never bothered me to fail in sports, because sports never interested me. Hell, I'm into video games and when someone else beats me, I don't get mad because I failed. At least I had fun.

I do get mad when I let myself down. I bombed big time in the local comedy club once. My audience that night was uppity white people. Most uppity white people with money don't dig jokes about abortion and semen. Jokes that had killed with college crowds didn't get a single laugh. As I decided I had had enough, I said, "That's my time, you've been a wonderful audience. Wait a second, what the fuck am I thinking? YOU ALL SUCKED!"

I think that line is the only reason I even tried standup comedy again. I had never heard a comedian tell his audience that they sucked. I was actually laughing about that as I was walking off the stage.

I was disappointed though, as I felt that I had failed at comedy. To make things worse, I had brought a friend along and he saw me fail. On the way home, he started giving me advice on how to do standup. I told him to shut the fuck up or I was going to hurt him. I do not need anyone who has never had the guts to stand in front of a crowd and tell jokes giving me advice on how to do it.

In grade school, I got a D in handwriting. Didn't bother me one bit, because I didn't care. I'm left-handed and my handwriting sucks. You don't like it? Tough shit, teacher. I'll just take my A in reading.

If I had gotten a D in reading, though, man, I'd have been pissed. I'm just not used to failing at things I'm good at, and I guess most people are like that. Failing at things I care about is pretty tough for me to deal with, though, yet there is usually no better teacher than failure. Behind every success story is a bunch of failures no one ever heard about.

I had failed in something much more important than reading or writing; I'd failed in love. It hurt to realize that. She never called me during the whole summer. I knew what that really meant. I was nothing to her, nothing more than a diversion. That pedestal I had placed her on was finally starting to crumble. I like to think that was because she was getting fatter.

In high school, I was a band geek. I had the choice between band

and art, so I chose band. I can't draw worth a fuck. I received a $500 scholarship from my high school band when I graduated. There was only one catch to it: I had to further my music education in college. To them, that meant "the recipient of this scholarship must take band in college." To me, that meant, "if I take two or three classes, I can get this scholarship."

I decided to take piano lessons and a music theory class. I hear this pissed off the donors of the scholarship, but what could they say? I followed the rules. The point is that she was in my music theory class. Pure coincidence. I would have never taken that class if I hadn't received the scholarship.

She was the only person I knew in the class, and I was the only person she knew in the class, so we sat next to each other. The class met twice a week, and we'd basically talk the whole time, as our teacher sucked. At this point, I still would have dated her if I had the chance, but I would have had next to no enthusiasm about it. Ok, maybe a little, but nowhere near the elation I would have had the previous year. I was still willing to be her friend, though, but I was pretty much over her.

And my archrival? He had started going to school. Funny. He put off a year of his life for her. He got an email account, and somehow we started emailing each other. I was curious about their relationship. They hung out together all the time! So, were they indeed a couple or not? That much, I really did want to know.

He told me that they were not a couple, which I just couldn't figure out at all. I even saw them holding hands once while walking around campus. He also asked me if I knew who Aragon from Arathon was (or some shit like that). I had never read the book, but I knew it was from *The Hobbit* by J.R.R. Tolkien. He was impressed. Of course, I may be wrong about the name. I don't read geek shit.

At least my suspicions were confirmed. They weren't a couple at all (after all, why would he lie to me?), and she wouldn't even give me one date. Cunt. Looking back, I really should have asked her out, and when she refused, I should have said, "And just why don't I deserve an hour or two of your time? Why is that asking too much?" Being nostalgic pisses me off sometimes.

Our music theory class met on her birthday, and I bought her a CD. Just a little gift to say, "I remembered." She thanked me. A few weeks later, I asked her what she thought of it, and she said, "It was a good CD. Too bad I lost it."

I believe part of the requirement of that class was that we had to go to a performance. That was fine, as there was a musical performance almost every night of the week. She tells me which one she is going to go to, and I tell her I'd go to that one too. Hey, I didn't want to sit by myself.

The concert started at 8:00. I got there at around 7:50. She wasn't there. Oh well, looks like I was going to be alone after all. At about 8:40, some people arrived through the back door. It's her, and she's with HIM, another guy, and a girl we both knew from our high school class together, Jennifer. Jennifer was a highly attractive girl who had gone off to school instead of staying in this city. She had only gone about 100 miles away, but I hadn't seen her for about seven months.

Looking back, I think Jennifer could see that I was a good guy and that I'm at least friendship material. My social life was very bad during high school. Quite a few upper-middle-class kids went to my high school because their parents couldn't afford private schools. Everyone, except about four people, was snobbish to me. I think it was because they knew I was really intelligent, while they were just pretending to be. I know that sounds snobbish of me, but it's seriously the only thing I could think of.

I took AP English with the snobs. That's when I learned that most of them were just pretending to be smart, but really weren't special. I took the AP English test, as did everyone else who signed up for AP English. There was one person who had gotten the highest score possible, a five. The snobs treated her even worse than they did me, as she was a "freak." I found her to be a very nice person. I look normal, though, so I was probably higher in the hierarchy of seniors. I got a four. There was only one other four, and the only person in my grade who I didn't think was pretending to be smart achieved that score. So, among so-called "smart people," there was only one five and two fours. Everyone else made a three or below, and they were supposedly "too good" to hang around with me.

Younger classmates loved me. When I was a senior, there were freshmen who knew my name and I didn't know theirs. I liked quite a few of these people, but they did every extra-curricular activity in the world, or they had church, or something. Sometimes hanging out was a matter of comparing their schedules (full) to mine (free).

I'm telling you this so you know I did no hanging out with anyone in high school outside of school. I went to school with a bunch of fucking dullards. I had friends' *parents* invite me to movies where my friends just wouldn't do that sort of thing. It was complete social hell. Before I moved to this place, I had an active social life. Now, I was stuck sitting in my room, watching television, and playing Sega.

When graduation came around, Jennifer came up to me and said, "What are you doing tonight?"

"Oh, I've got to call some friends and family and blah blah blah." I don't remember what I said.

I'm driving home from graduation, and it fucking hits me! "Jennifer was asking if you wanted to go out with her tonight! You stupid shit!"

I was devastated that I didn't catch on to that. I had not been invited anywhere by fellow classmates for years. The one time I am, I didn't catch on, and it must have seemed to her like I blew her off! Christ!

I didn't even have her phone number to arrange something for a later date.

Jennifer was a friend to both her and me. When it came to choosing one of us, Jennifer chose her instead of me. Well, of course. She couldn't keep in touch with both of us. That would be wrong and awkward.

Still, though, it was refreshing to see Jennifer, even if *she* was with her. Of course, *she* didn't think to look for me when picking a seat. *She* just walked in and picked four seats that were together.

Bitch.

There was a 10-minute intermission. As soon as it was announced, the four of them got up to leave. I could tell by how they were leaving that they were not going to come back. Well, I can see her anytime, but Jennifer was a different story. Since I was closer to the back door than they were, I arrived at the lobby before they did.

Jennifer was leading them out of the auditorium. When Jen came through that door and saw me standing there, a huge smile appeared on her face. She ran over and hugged me and asked me how I was doing. She told me it was great to see me again, and then *she* interrupted us.

"C'mon Jennifer, we have to go," she coldly said.

They weren't going to any place important. I think they were going out to eat, if memory serves me right. And I could see it in her eyes and mannerisms—Jennifer wanted me to go with them, but knew it would offend the ex-chick-of-my-dreams if she had invited me.

I said goodbye to Jennifer. It was the last time I ever saw her. I walked into the auditorium, and for the first time in my life, I was mad at that bitch. How dare she keep me from talking to someone I hadn't seen for over six months!

I was never particularly warm towards her again. I talked to her in class, but kept it at a bare minimum. She had made a choice. She chose to treat me like five-day-old dog shit: She couldn't even smell me, thus she could ignore me completely. What the fuck did I ever do to her? Oh yeah, I showed her kindness, loyalty, and tried to be her friend.

She made her choice, so now I made my choice. I could keep talking to her, or I could never give a fuck about her again. I chose the latter.

After that, I only saw her sporadically. I said hi and always asked her how she was, but of course I didn't really care.

Once I saw her and she told me she was failing her psychology class. I wound up taking the same class a few semesters later and I don't see how anyone could fail it if they showed up every day. It was practically impossible to fail the class. You could get a B if you listened.

The next semester, I ran into a high-school friend of mine who told me that he was in a psychology class with her. Interesting, huh? She had indeed failed, and was retaking the course. He then told me that she hardly ever showed up for class. She'd show up maybe once a week, if that, according to him.

Wow. She was becoming a loser. Hey, I know college life isn't for everyone, yet I just can't fathom why someone would spend money on their classes and books and not show up. That shows disrespect for the money used to pay for their education.

She eventually told me she was going to go to nursing school.

*   *   *

I haven't seen her in almost three years. I just realized that. That's pretty amazing, because I can still picture her face in my mind. In some way, she's permanently a part of me. That sucks, huh?

When that pedestal on which I had placed her started crumbling, it crumbled rapidly and broke into a billion pieces. She had gained that much weight, I'm afraid. Poor pedestal couldn't take any more pressure.

Seriously, though, I just started seeing all these faults in her. I didn't want someone who was going to waste their money on college classes that they weren't going to attend. What does that say about a person? It's one thing to not go to a class and pass it, another to not go to a class and fail it, yet another to fail a class because you skipped it and then retake it, only to skip it again. I started to picture her living in a trailer park 20 years from now. I really thought she was going to grow up to become trailer trash, or at least poor. Not that being rich is good and being poor is bad, it's just that money is an important thing, and it's much easier to be happy when you don't have to worry about money.

She also couldn't at least be a friend to me. I still despise her for that. I would not have minded being in the "friend zone" one bit. I had virtually no friends when I started college, because most of my friends were in high school, and they were a bunch of dweebs. They didn't keep in touch at all. I knew who my true friends were, and I had only one in this city. I spent many Friday nights at home alone, because getting drunk at frat parties and bars just wasn't my thing. I tried to meet people in classes, but I had a predominately male major at the time, and I didn't particularly care for most of the other students in my major. Having a few more friends would have really helped me. Again, I am to take most of the blame for this myself, because I chose to stay home on those Friday nights. However, I do harbor resentment towards her and a few others, for not being my friend, which brings me to my next point.

Remember the business about that message I sent to her in high school about me throwing up on her? She had gotten the message and I didn't know it. The next day, she treated me like shit, and Monday, when she was supposed to have gotten the message, she didn't say a word about it. In fact, she never said a word about it at all. So in my mind, she never got the message.

After HE showed me the message, I felt really bad. I had obviously pissed her off. I called her up and told her to be honest with me. I told her I never knew she got the message, and it really sucked for her to just give me the cold shoulder and not even discuss things with me. She didn't even give me a chance to defend myself.

Of course, not telling me she was pissed and just sending me bad vibes instead is a woman thing. That's just how women communicate. I, being male, am much smarter than she is, thus I have the ability to read minds. Yes, I can communicate telepathically. I should just *know* both when and why someone is mad at me.

I also learned that getting in good with a chick's parents is death when it comes to courting a chick. Her parents were divorced, which screwed both her and her brother up big time. Her brother was a huge druggie, probably has little future ahead of him if he hasn't straightened up yet. She was fucking up her future by not being patient enough to survive a few years of college. Hell, if anyone should have dropped out of college, it should have been me! I had gotten some incredible job offers in California, and had to turn them all down because I was still in school. So, not only did she not make it through school, but she also had a chance to be with me, and didn't take it.

But her mom knew I had the potential to not only be a provider for her daughter, but to also make her daughter a very happy woman. And of course, if her mother said, "Why don't you give him a chance, I think it's sweet how much he obviously likes you," well, then I'd have better luck finding a porno with a chick that looks something like her than actually getting a date with her.

I've not seen her in almost three years, but of course, I am omniscient. I can tell you that she's now married. Yes, she was just one month younger than me, yet she is married, at 23. She got pregnant. She has already given birth. My calculations determine that she got pregnant when she was 21, possibly even before that. The guy she married wasn't too bright, was majorly sexist, but of course he wasn't bad-looking so girls could never see anything bad about him. My sister was shocked when she found out whom my first true love married. Incidentally, he was the fourth person who attended the concert with Jennifer, my first true love, and HIM. They still hang together after all these years, and they completely ignore me. Wonderful.

The guy she married is in the army, so she lives with him in a rural area of this state. That is, if he isn't in Somalia or some shit like that. Not to knock everyone in the army, but really, there are quite a few losers who join the army just because they know if they don't, they won't be able to get a job anywhere else. The army only has fitness standards. If you can sign your name and do 25 pushups, you're in.

When she inquired about me, she was told that I have been dating a girl for a while, and that I will either be moving to New York or California. The woman I'm dating wants to get married before I move away, but I really don't want to get married. I don't know what her reaction was to that. I was told that she appeared to be very happy with her life and her daughter, but of course, appearances can be deceiving. My girlfriend Amy can be pissed as hell at me, yet she will be nice as can be to someone who walks in on us while we're fighting.

Of course, there is a possibility that my ex-goddess-on-a-pedestal really is happy with her life. I think that's terrific. And I really hope she is happy living in a trailer being a mommy with a kid holding her back and a husband who will grow tired of her and probably womanize (after all, he's in the army, you know), or better yet, he'll get killed in a war and she'll be all alone, while I'm enjoying a luxurious lifestyle in New York or California, taking in culture and art and enjoying my youth, and even enjoying my job, until I finally settle down and have a family when I'm responsible enough to afford to provide for my wife and child(ren) so I can give them the best life possible.

I don't care if I ever see her again, but I wish I could know when she thinks about me. I wish I could know if she will ever regret treating me the way she did. I regret being as nice to her as I was.

She didn't deserve it.

I know this story isn't special. It's happened to a million guys like me. It will happen to a million more. I wish there was a way to teach young men who fall in love with someone who doesn't appreciate them how to tell if they aren't going to get the girl. There was never any doubt in my mind during my senior year of high school. I was going to win. I was going to get with her, probably even marry her, and live a happy, fulfilling life.

Fucking television sitcoms feeding trash to my brain. If I ever see *Mr. Belvedere* or *Growing Pains* again, I'm going to shoot my television.

CHAPTER 3

HER Analysis

She was my first love. She taught me a lot about how fucked up chicks really are. This isn't really so much about what I did wrong, but what I learned from the experiences with her.

I made references to the pedestal I put her on. Never, *ever*, put another person on a pedestal, *especially not a chick*. This goes for people too—a boss, a celebrity, whoever. Everyone's biological functions are the same. Everyone has a beating heart. Everyone hates rapper Eminem. Some things are just universal. Therefore, there isn't a soul on the planet who deserves to be worshipped in any way, *especially not a chick*. If you find yourself worshipping a chick, STOP! She's not fucking worth it. A billion men have had the same experiences that I've had with HER, and I gotta tell you, it never goes your way. I would have been so much wiser if I had known someone who had been there and done that.

When I found out I made her mad at me over that stupid card I wrote her (the one that HE called me on, asking why I gave that to her), I was physically ill. I even came close to vomiting a few times. Ugh. If I could only go back and shoot myself over and over, revive myself, and shoot myself again. But I don't have to do that, because I started thinking about it immediately after wiping the spit from the rim of the toilet. SHE just *expected me* to know not only that she was mad at me, but why she was mad at me as well.

I could figure out that she was mad at me. That was a no-brainer. However, I was stumped as to why. As I said, I thought she was on the rag. I didn't find out for another month or so why she was really mad at me, and I'm actually lucky to have found out at all.

Chicks are beyond stupid. I mean, how many times have you guys ever thought that someone else knew exactly why you were mad at them without telling them? Sure, Joe knows we're mad at him . . . we told him why. For some reason, chicks just think we ought to know why they're giving us the freezing cold shoulder. Is it any wonder that it's women who call the fucking Psychic Hotline for $6 a minute?

My friends constantly brought me up to her, and while I know they were trying to help me, I should have told them to stop it. However, this is a very minor mistake, because I was never going to get with her anyway. In reality, I had nothing to lose, so why not make her as miserable as me?

Another thing I learned: High-school males—if your "crush's" parents love you to death, you're going to be lucky to even get a hug. Stop right away. You're doomed. It's not going to happen. You'll have a better chance of fucking her mom.

I also learned that guys have a huge ability to take tons of shit and just be completely blinded. I swore for a year I was going to get the girl. I didn't. Luckily, I opened my eyes and realized that she wasn't that great, and in fact she had quite a few problems.

Another mistake: I never gave away her name. I should have used her real name in this book so she could know my true feelings. However, she doesn't deserve the fame, and she missed her chance. She will never have the opportunity to boink me.

CHAPTER 4

The Two Types of Chicks

There are two types of chicks—time whores and money whores. There may be a third type of chick, and maybe even a fourth, but let's explore the other two first.

Money whores—I firmly believe the majority of chicks are money whores. Oh, sure, most won't admit they are no matter what. Just like with serial killers and rapists, you can't believe everything a chick says. No. It's her behavior that you must look at, not her fat trap.

Fame, to chicks, is money. And even the late "comedian" (I put that in quotes because I didn't find him funny) Chris Farley, who weighed about 800 lbs, got laid regularly. Rush Limbaugh? When he was 300 lbs., he met his future wife. I never saw her, but she was supposedly a fitness instructor from a college in Florida. Anyhow, she fell in love with him, but poor old Rush's money and fame wasn't good enough. She made him lose like 150 lbs. or something.

But the fact is, Rush got laid from a sexy coed, and in Rush's case, that's astounding. Not only is the guy fat, but he's also a die-hard Republican. I haven't seen many hot Republican chicks. Something tells me Orwin Hatch's wife isn't a hottie.

Rosie O'Donnell. Roseanne Barr. The only guy that would sleep with Roseanne Barr was Tom Arnold, and that alone got him famous. He deserves it too, as I'm sure sleeping with Roseanne couldn't have been fun. Hell, even after Roseanne got her stomach stapled, and consequently lost a lot of weight, she **still** can't get hot guys to date her.

It doesn't work both ways. Even the most desperate of guys still won't go for ugly famous chicks.

So, any chick that marries a rich guy is a whore. Any chick. Even if she was dating him before he was rich. Most chicks don't want to work; they want to shop and watch "their shows." Most chicks want to be treated like princesses or queens, and that takes money.

Any chick who says, "You couldn't afford me," to a guy propositioning her is a money whore (duh). I wish I could be insanely attractive to women one day, and when I'm asked out, I'd say, "You couldn't afford me."

At one time, it was acceptable to be a money whore, and actually it was the norm. But now women want equal pay for equal work, and men have to put up with that, and the fact is that most women still want a guy to provide for them, even if they're working. It's a double standard that feminism has brought upon us. "We want the same money for the same work, making it harder for you to afford me."

One of my readers told me comedian Bill Maher said something like, "A guy has to go through school, make good grades, get into college, work hard for four years, get a degree, get a high-paying job and get a nice car to impress the opposite sex. Women have to do their hair."

Believe me, some guys want to get laid so badly that they really will work that hard. Do you think anyone *really* wants to become a medical doctor? Hell no! But the pay is wonderful, and of course, you'll get chicks if you have money.

A lot of chicks wonder why so many guys don't respect women. It's simple: Most women have done nothing to earn respect.

I would love to be famous, just for a few days, so I could see the difference in how chicks treated me. I know guys would treat me differently too, but chicks would be so much different. They'd let their whoreness show through. And I, of course, would have no respect for almost all of them.

The plus of being with a money whore is that because they're so superficial, she's a trophy. You can go anywhere with her and be the envy of most guys. I imagine it's quite a cool feeling.

The minus is that she may make you go bankrupt, and you probably don't love her that much, so she may not be worth the money.

The second type of chick is the time whore. There are quite a few of these around. In fact, The Chicks Suck Guy's Law of Whorativity states: "If she's not a money whore, then she's a time whore."

When I use the term "time whore," I'm not talking specifically about clingy chicks, although they do fall into this category. Clingy chicks are the worst: They practically throw themselves all over a guy, which may be cool to the guy for the first day. After that, it's annoying as hell, and the chick wonders why nobody will stay with her for more than a month.

The non-clingy time whore describes a lot of chicks. Amy is this type of time whore. She's not clingy, but she has a need to be around me almost every day. It's fine with me, because I like her a lot and we don't get too annoyed with each other, but it also sucks, because sometimes I think we get into fights solely because we're around each other so much.

She also puts me in the position of having to choose between work and her. I do a lot of work at home, and she'll be there, and she'll say, "When are you going to be done?" even though I've told her it's going to be a while and I don't know. Although it was annoying, I got used to it, so it wasn't a big deal.

However, I did stop updating the site for quite a while, just because I never had anything to talk about. She was always there, and since she wanted me to be with her, either watching TV or going out somewhere, I'd choose her over the site (which is the right choice, I might add).

There are many benefits to being with a time whore. They are cheaper than money whores, and they don't mind if you spend your money on things you like, as they usually benefit from them too. I purchased a 36" Sony Wega Television, and of course, Amy loves it. Because you're around each other all the time, you get used to things, and you may even start to like things about her that you didn't like at first. You grow and share experiences together, and you want to do almost everything with (and to) her.

Those can also be minuses. If you want her to do something she doesn't want to, like anal sex, it can be a problem. If you don't want to do something that she wants you to—also a problem. Especially since she can say, "I let you have anal sex and I didn't want to, so you have to go with me to my grandma's, since you don't want to." If she comes over to your place more often, expect that to be used against you. If you've got work to do, you're going to have to nicely let her down. And after a long night of work, you may be tired, and she has been waiting for sex, and all you want to do is go to bed. Problem indeed.

The biggest problem, though, is that you get used to her being there all the time, and if you ever have to be apart for a few months, you're miserable. You become as dependent on her as she is on you. If you ever have to choose to put the relationship on hold while you pursue your dreams, it makes things much more complicated than they otherwise would have been.

There is a third type of chick—both at once! Yes, combine a time whore and a money whore and you've got to get away from her quickly! There are a few of these, so be very, very careful.

The fourth type of chick probably doesn't exist, and that's neither a time whore nor a money whore. If you find one of these, you've hit the jackpot. She'll do what you want, when you want, but that may not fulfill you. Believe it or not, conflict can be good. Or, she can be the type that wants to provide for herself, and only wants a man for companionship. In this case, that's a sure thing, and it's usually the type of chick I, and most men, are attracted to most. Someone who doesn't need us, yet wants us there. Awesome.

Obviously, the question here is, "Are all chicks whores?" Flip the page for the answer.

CHAPTER 5

Are All Chicks Whores?

I've said that there are basically two types of women: time whores and money whores. So I'm sure most of you are asking: "Chicks Suck Guy, do you think all women are whores?"

I think most, if not all, women are whores. Most women do not freely sleep with any guy; they have "standards." Since a guy has to meet those "standards" to sleep with them, that makes the majority of chicks whores.

Of what kind of standards do I speak? Is it that the guy has to have a job and not live with his parents if he's older than 25? Is it that the guy has to speak English? Is it that he has to be breathing? Or does he just have to be human?

No. That's not what I'm talking about, nimrod. Obviously, we all have standards. I don't want a chick I fuck to have an STD. I want a chick I fuck to be well-groomed, or at least not smell.

Those are reasonable standards. But we're talking about chicks here; hence we must throw out all logic. And most chicks' "standards" exclude the majority of men.

If you don't believe me, read personal ads on the Web or the local newspaper. When I first found out about Web personal ads, I was instantly attracted to the idea. An easy way to meet chicks. Wonderful. Well, I started going to them, and now I'm attracted to them not because I want to meet someone, but because I can't believe what women actually put in an ad.

Some guys put in stuff like, "27 yo WM, just wants to fuck." Good for him. He's honest and simple. Let me quote a few unedited ads that some of the local chicks have posted. (And let me stress, I did not make these up. These are real.)

Ad #1:
Title: Are there any real men left?
Hi I'm 29 and have been seperated for quite awhile.
I'am looking for someone that wants to sweep me off
my feet and treat me like a queen and in return you
will be treated like a king. You have to love children
for I have 2 daughters and hope to have a son one
day. I love horses and hiking and movies and music.
You must be sincere and attractive and compassion-
ate towards those around you. Life is about helping
people cause you never know when you will need
someone. I dont take life too seriously but there
comes a time when you have to stand up for what is
right. Like the song says 'you got to stand for som-
thing or you will fall for anything.' I'm not into games.
Life is too short and people arent meant to be played
with. I'am looking for something long term so if you
arent please dont waste my time. If you are over-
weight dont respond. Physical chemistry is very important. I'm no Cindy Crawford but I'am an attractive
lady. I have been told many times that I look like
Courtney Cox from Friends and the movie Scream. I
prefer a non smoker but occasional smokers is okay. I
enjoy the simple things in life and you have to. I'm
pretty old fashioned but know how to make a man
feel like a man. If you still believe in bringing flowers
home for no reasong and leaving love notes for her
then please drop me a line and a photo. I hope you
are my soulmate. Thanks for reading my ad

Note: She's 5'3" and weighs 104 lbs.

I wonder who responded to this one.

"Hi, I saw your ad, and I instantly knew I had to write

you. I've been looking for someone who I can worship, but at the same time knows how to make me feel like a real man. I am attractive, although my doctor told me that I'm 10 pounds overweight, but life is too short, so I enjoy the simple things. Like you, I'm old-fashioned too, since I don't have any kids and am not divorced. Well, I hope you like me so far, and I hope my weight isn't a problem. Life is short, but it can seem like an eternity when you've got two kids and aren't married and need someone to shower you with flowers so you can feel special. I'd like to see the guy who was lucky enough to drop his seed into your twat twice. At least he wasn't overweight. You say you want a real man, yet 'real men' have beer guts, don't you know that? Only pansies work out."

Ad #2:
Title: SugarDaddy
This may sound far fetched, but what the heck! I am a single mother of two kids. I work my fingers to the bone! I am so tired by the end of the day there is no time left for me. It is making me old before my time. I am looking for a man who is financially well off, kind and caring to take care of me and my kids. Someone to give us the life we deserve. Someone to treat me like a queen. I'm a attractive and intellegent woman who is alot of fun and who has a lot of love to give. If you are interested, send me an email. Enclose a pic and i will respond.

Note: She's 5'7" and weighs 160 lbs.

Well, boys, we have a winner here, huh? Not only does the title of her ad show she's a fucking whore, but we can't have her get old now, can we? She *deserves* better, even though she's spread her legs twice. She had nothing to do with herself getting pregnant and being stuck in a one-way job. She probably plays the lottery believing she's going to hit it big. C'mon guys, there's a lot of opportunity here. Why, while you're dating her, she may hit Megabucks. I also love it when people write that they are intelligent, and MISSPELL THE FUCKING WORD. That's really attractive. But the best thing is that she wants a guy financially well off to take care of her and her kids. Well shit! That's why I went to college! To date a leech like this chick! Hey, I'll buy your kids some shoes if you'll let me inside of you! C'mon whore! Suck my dick and your kids get a new wardrobe!

Ad #3:
Title: Southern Beauty.
I believe in love and everything that comes with it. I'm seeking someone who believes in and truly wants to fall in love. I'm 23 and am kept extremely busy in the retail world. I love Harleys ,riding,movies, candlelit dinners, good conversation (I never have a lack of words), Vegas, dancing. I'm extremely energetic and ambitious. I prefer to live my life like 'Friends'based on laughter and fun and not be a drama like 'The Practice.' I love romantic comedies and would prefer my dating life to be the same. I'm seeking a male,over 18. Must be fun,secure. I'm seeking a career minded, goal minded guy who would like a friend and maybe more . I'm seeking a guy who's responsible, but knows how to laugh and be a kid. I'm seeking a guy who likes to hold hands, cuddle and spend time getting to know me. Very importantly, Please email me and tell me about yourself. To learn more about me,email me I also have a photo or 2 on request . . . .

Note: She's 5'8" and weighs 130 lbs.

This one seems like the most innocent, but the guys out there already know she's just as shallow as the chicks in the other two ads. In the chapter where I talk about how much influence television had on my life, I at least figured out that television wasn't like real life, even when it came to love. This chick has yet to figure that out. She wants her dating life to be like a romantic comedy, and not some stupid drama. More like *Friends* because real life should be more like *Friends*, I'm sure we'd all agree with that one. She wants a career-minded, goal-minded guy because she's just a cashier who isn't going to go anywhere (certainly not to school) anytime soon, and besides, school isn't fun, it's more like *The Practice* than *Friends*, and of course we must be entertained every second of our miserable lives, even when we're cashiering at Spencer's Gifts at the fucking mall.

All of the chickies above have standards—unreasonable ones. Hey "ladies," if you've got any kids, you ought to thank your lucky stars that you can even *get* a date. Guys want nothing to do with a chick who has a kid. When I was 14 years old, I considered myself a very giving person, but even then, I actually thought this: I would never go out with a woman with a kid. I'm nice, but I'm not going to raise anyone else's mistake.

The chicks above have unreasonable standards. All of them. "My life has to be like a sitcom, so if you aren't wacky or zany, you won't get pussy. You probably will get led to believe that I like you when I don't, because *that's* funny!"

You just saw, "I want a guy to treat me like a princess," and not, "I want a guy with whom I can have long intelligent conversations." Looking at personal ads in the South is even worse, because every other ad is titled, "Southern Belle," "Southern Beauty," or "Southern Princess." Blech.

They're whores, and those were just three random ads I saw. You can go to any personal ads Web site, or read the paper, and see the exact same things.

I don't want royalty. No guy wants royalty. I just want to have a partner in whom I can confide and with whom I can have fun. Someone who is willing to put as much into a relationship as I am. If things don't work out romantically while we're dating, I'm not opposed to being friends, as one can never have too many. Those are realistic standards. I don't care if she's taller than me, has red hair or brown hair, or "unattractive" by today's standards. Attractiveness does not a relationship make.

To be fair, I did check out the men seeking women ads, and a few were, "I've got my own business, and I like to travel and go scuba diving." They were posted by 40+-year-old guys searching for 20-year-old girls. And I'm sure those money whores responded immediately. Aside from that, most of the ads I've seen haven't been very specific, but the ones that were basically said, "I'd like someone to hang out with for a little bit." I've never seen the male equivalent of the ads I listed above. What would the male equivalent look like?

> Title: Seeking busty model to suck my cock.
> Hey ladies, how's it going? Thanks for reading my ad. I'm work in management for a multi-million-dollar company—McDonald's. And I'm looking for some nice girls to fuck. You've got to have blonde hair and at least be a D cup. If you are less than 5'5" tall, you can forget about being with me. I just like to be real, that's all, and flipping burgers all day gives you a chance to really think about what you want out of life. If you're between 5'5" and 5'8", you can't weigh more than 145 lbs. And you must be willing to swallow. Oh, my car got impounded the other day, so I can't really drive to meet you. You'll have to pick me up at my place. Don't worry, though, when we go out to eat, I can get free food. Being in management has its privaliges! You don't have to be willing to give me anal sex, but that's a plus!

While that character is merely a figment of my imagination, something tells me that even if he did exist, he'd never write that ad. Something tells me that he'd be getting laid regularly. In fact, he'd probably be the father of ad #2's two kids.

The point of this chapter isn't how stupid chicks are in personal ads; it's just to show their way of thinking. These ads demonstrate what the nice woman you just met is really thinking. Believe me, they reflect the norm and not the fringe. Through these ads, it's easy to tell most women are whores. They have completely unreasonable standards, except when a guy with a cute butt walks by. So, either be a gentleman who will raise two kids, or have a cute butt. If you can, have the cute butt and forget being a gentleman. You won't have to stick around.

CHAPTER 6

The Grass is Always Greener. . .

If there is one law that is constant in all of human psychology, it's that the grass is always greener on the other side of the fence. We all want what we can't have. If only I had a million dollars . . . If only I were as smart as him . . . I wish I could be as beautiful as her . . . I wish I could be famous. My life would be better if <fill in the blank>.

Just look at Bill Gates. He had the business savvy to go from being a college dropout to being the world's richest man. And you know what? That's still not good enough. Bill Gates doesn't have to work another day in his life, yet he does. He writes a newspaper column. He still has a lot of control at Microsoft. If he died tomorrow, he would go down in history as one of the revolutionaries of the Information Age. His name will mean to the people in the next century what names like John D. Rockefeller and Andrew Carnegie mean to us now.

That's not good enough, though. There's still more for Bill Gates to do. He constantly wants to improve Microsoft's software. He still doesn't have what he wants. He wants more.

Of course, the same goes for all of us. We want more. It's true for dating, mating, and marriage, and it's especially true for men. It's the real reason we fear commitment. "Is this girl really the girl for me? Maybe there's someone else who would be better."

On my Web site, I wrote about non-married monogamy. I think it's ridiculous that people who go out with each other for one or two months are "exclusive" to each other. What bullshit! That would mean that if I go out for someone for a year, and it doesn't work out, I have literally missed out on one year of opportunities. I may have even missed the elusive "one." You know, that "one" who was made just for me. The "one" I have spent my whole life looking for. The "one" who probably doesn't even exist.

I have more of an open relationship with Amy than most people have with their girlfriends. If I see a chick I want to fuck, and I fuck her, it's okay with Amy as long as I tell her that I had sex with a chick. Amy says that it's just fine for me to explore my sexuality with someone else if I wear a condom and as long as she knows about it. The same goes for Amy, though. If she sees a hot chick she wants to fuck, it's okay as long as she tells me and wears a condom. We can both fuck chicks. Why should I be allowed to have a double standard?

But talk about freedom, huh? Getting to fuck other chicks with just two tiny stipulations? And I bet a bunch of guys out there think I have it made. I hit the jackpot. The grass is greener on my side of the fence.

In a way, I'm very lucky to have someone who lets me be free, so to speak. I don't have the ball-and-chain that many men do.

I have a theory that if we legalized pot, fewer people would want to smoke it. When I was a kid, maybe five years old, my father said I could drink anything I wanted. As long as I did it in the home, I could get plastered. (My dad is Irish, as if you had to even ask.) In one of my earliest memories, I remember drinking a Guinness he poured me with my breakfast of Strawberry Shortcake cereal before catching the bus to kindergarten.

As I grew older, I never drank. When I was 13 years old, I told my friends that I could drink if I wanted to. They envied me. That was so cool to them. But you know what? I didn't want to. Drinking had no appeal to me. If you tell a kid to never go into daddy's sock drawer, that kid will do so as soon as he gets the chance. If you don't tell him that, he may accidentally stumble upon some porn one day. You're much better off not even mentioning daddy's sock drawer. As soon as daddy's sock drawer is off-limits, Junior is going to wonder why.

But, of course, that's drugs, porn, and alcohol. I'm talking about pussy. Amy says I can go after it, and even indulge in it, and as long as I tell her about it, that's fine. Unlike alcohol, as soon as it is offered to me, I'm going to take it. Pussy may be an abundant resource on the planet, but it's not abundant in my life, and it's certainly not as abundant as alcohol.

I still have a conscience, though. I am still obligated to Amy no matter what. Even though my leash is loose, I still have a leash. I made my own leash. What I mean is, if I got some new pussy, I'd definitely tell Amy because if I didn't, I'd be riddled with guilt.

In one of my classes last semester, there was a girl who just drove me wild. I was attracted to her the very first moment I saw her. I don't get that kind of attraction for most people. Usually, I get that kind of attraction after talking to an intelligent chick for a little bit, but I got this thought like, "Wow!" when I first saw her. She had olive-colored skin, shoulder-length black hair with a blond streak going down the side. Most men would say she was just cute, but she really turned me on. She was definitely my type. Well, her looks were, anyway.

The class was a tough class. It met two times a week. At first she would show up once a week. As it got more difficult, she showed up more regularly. One day she was wearing a shirt that showed off her cleavage, and she was across the room, but in my field of view. Every time she bent over to pick something up, I had a full view of her tits. I had a huge fucking boner by the end of class that day.

I didn't really tell Amy about her, though. I didn't know her name, for one. Also, there was nothing to tell. I think a chick in my class is hot. Really hot. Not much more to talk about there.

I shared a post office box with a friend of mine who moved. He subscribed to *Maxim* magazine. On a side note, I think they ought to change the name of *Maxim* to "How To Get Laid Magazine, written by ugly guys and creative girls who think the fact that men believe this shit is funny." *Maxim* probably would not have been a success if they had called it that, though. Anyhow, since my friend moved, I now get his issues of *Maxim*.

Amy loves to read *Maxim*. She finds it funny and interesting. She finds me funny and interesting too, so that probably explains why she likes *Maxim*. One night, she read *Maxim*'s interview with Melissa Joan Hart, the chick who plays Sabrina on *Sabrina The Teenage Witch*, and more importantly Clarissa from Nickelodeon's now defunct *Clarissa Explains It All*.

Amy read me a part of the interview.

"They asked her what her favorite pickup line is. She replied, 'Don't I know you from somewhere?'"

Fucking chicks. Guys have to have creative pickup lines. Not chicks. The most generic and unoriginal pickup lines work for them, because they have pussy. Pussy is more valuable than gold, although if you have enough gold, getting pussy is usually not a problem.

The next day, I was in class with hot chick. At the end of class she asked me, "Aren't you in one of my other classes?"

A variation on Melissa Joan Hart's pickup line! Holy shit! If there was anything I had learned from my Web site, it was to act interested in the most disinterested way I could. I wasn't going to screw this one up.

"Not this semester. Maybe you were last semester, but I don't remember."

This showed her that while I had noticed her this semester, I really didn't have a clue about last semester. (Of course, we both knew that we had never seen each other before.) Since I don't show interest in her, she automatically wants me more. Why? Because we all want what we can't have. Because the grass is always greener . . .

I wound up walking her to her car in the parking lot, and I scored her name and phone number. Wow. I was psyched. Here is a chick that I thought was extremely hot who struck up a conversation with me, and I got her name, Andrea, and even her digits! Damn, this was looking great! She also used a pickup line on me. Shit.

I told Amy about it, and Amy was fine with it. Wow. Maybe she did really mean what she said. After all, people have a way of talking about how they would act in hypothetical situations, and acting completely different when those hypothetical situations cease to be hypothetical.

Fortunately, Amy seemed to be okay with it. I had been with Amy for a year and a half, and had almost complete freedom during that time. Finally, it looked like I had a chance to enjoy some of that freedom. Maybe that's what Mel Gibson was screaming about in Braveheart.

Andrea wound up calling me a few times. Sometimes it seemed as if she was calling me for no reason. Once she called while Amy was over, and Amy was quiet so Andrea wouldn't think anyone else was in my room. Damn, that impressed me.

Amy is a time whore. Andrea, on the other hand, was a full-time student taking 18 hours, and she worked five eight-hour days a week, from 2pm to 11pm. The grass was starting to look greener to me. If I could get Andrea, I wouldn't have to spend too much time with her. I'm more of a loner, and sometimes I feel like I'm not as creative because I spend all of my time with Amy. I've told Amy that, but it's not like I'm blaming her or anything. It's my choice. I choose to spend most of my time with Amy.

I was amazed that Andrea called for no reason. Hardly anyone had ever used me before and actually cared to keep in touch. I've helped numerous people with numerous things since I've been in college, being pretty careful not to be too helpful. If you help people too much, they think you're a freak.

I was also amazed that Amy was quiet while I talked to Andrea. I started asking Amy a bunch of questions about my feelings. "What if I like her more than you?" "What happens if we break up over this?" "Will you regret your decision to let me pursue her?" Notice my positive tone. "Of course there is a huge chance I'll like her more," could easily be an underlying message of those questions.

Amy replied, "Look, I know you'll like me better. I've never been so sure of anything in my life. I know that if you get to know her, you'll see I'm the better person."

I admired Amy's confidence, but really, how could she possibly know that? And what about me? What if I did wind up liking Andrea more? How could I handle choosing Amy over Andrea? Yes, I'd be happy that the one girl I noticed this semester was with me, but I'm also pretty loyal, and I'd feel like crap about Amy. And I know it'd hurt her, big time. Do I even know what I'd do? How can Amy know that I'll like her more than Andrea if I don't even know?

"I know you're happy with me, and if it takes Andrea to show you that, that's fine," Amy said.

"Yes, and I know I'm happy with you, but maybe I could be happier with her," I said. Amy understood. Andrea's grass is sure looking green, huh? It's probably brunette, though, as Andrea does have dark hair.

Amy told me that she was afraid of me putting this chick on a pedestal and getting hurt by her. I'm no different than anyone else. When I'm infatuated with someone, I don't see any of their flaws. There's an old adage that says masturbation will make you blind. No. Pussy does that. Masturbation, more often than not, helps you see things clearly.

Andrea was absent from one class. It just happened to be the class where the teacher gave out the review sheets for the last exam. I, being the thoughtful nice guy that I am, took two. I gave Andrea a call that night and told her she missed the review sheet. She offered to stop by my work the next day and pick it up. I had no problem with that. I figured I'd nonchalantly ask her to lunch when she stopped by. The next day, I got a call from her saying that she had run into our teacher and he gave her a review sheet, so there was no need to stop by my job, thus it looked like I didn't have a lunch partner that day. Shit. Eating alone sucks. (Remember that I made plans to ask her out to lunch. I discuss it in the next chapter.)

Andrea was taking some college math class, and she said the teacher sucked. The teacher had them buy graphing calculators that he didn't even know how to use. They never used the calculators in class. I'd have been steamed if I had been in that class.

For her final, Andrea had a take-home math test. Following one of my rules on how not to get laid, I offered to help her out. While I'm no math whiz, I do remember more of that shit than I care to admit.

She asked me what she could do to repay me. At first, I said, "Nothing, really," but knew that wasn't the way to go. It would have been great if I had said, "A blowjob would suffice," but I couldn't, even jokingly. I didn't want to screw anything up. She said she'd have to take me to lunch or something. I said, "Lunch is fine, or you could just wear a shirt that says '<My Name> is the greatest person on the planet.'"

When I met her the next day, I told her lunch would be fine. She smiled when she saw me and I smiled when I saw her. To me, it was a smile of, "It's great to see you." That was what my smile said, anyway. I sat down on a couch with her, and she was explaining stuff to me and all I could think was, "This girl is absolutely gorgeous."

She needed to meet with a guy in her class too, so we went to the math building and found him and I started helping him out as well. I had to leave early, and she walked me to the door and told me thank you. She really did appreciate me. I could tell. And she was polite about it. And she owed me lunch. Things were looking good with Andrea.

Amy and I have also been fighting recently. We used to fight maybe once every three months, and now it seems like we're fighting once every three days. And these are heavy fights. We yell and scream. We usually resolve the problem, but not without being pissed off at each other.

While Andrea had nothing to do with our fights, every time we fought, I would think about how nice it could be to start anew. I was getting tired of fighting constantly. Maybe some space apart would actually help Amy and me.

I helped Andrea on her math ten days ago. (No, I didn't know "ten days" off the top of my head.) She hasn't called me once since then. I did call her twice about the final in the class we had together, so I really can't hold that against her. The holidays are also coming up, and I understand how things can get hectic. Besides, all she owes me is lunch. However, I also don't want her to forget that she owes me lunch.

Amy and I got into a huge fight tonight. She wound up hanging up the phone on me, and it happened to be about the same time Andrea usually gets home. Perfect. I could talk to her and maybe feel a bit better. I could even redeem that imaginary "free lunch with Andrea" card I had. And how did our conversation go?

"Hello?"

"Hey Andrea, it's <My Name>, how are you doing?"

"I'm fine and how are you?" she cheerfully asked.

"I'm good. I'm calling because I was going through my records and I noticed that you still owe me lunch . . ."

"*sigh*"

"Well, you don't sound too excited about *that*," I said, and boy was I pissed.

She explained that she'd been really busy and that all she'd done was gone shopping for people. We talked for 10 or 15 minutes, and she sounded really tired, so I told her I'd call her back some other time and "redeem my lunch."

While I wasn't hurt, I was a bit disappointed. She fucking sighed. Maybe she was really tired. Maybe she was mad at her dogs. More than likely, she didn't want to hear from me at that moment in time. While I can understand that, there are better ways to say it than sighing into the phone. At least pretend to have something better to do than go out to eat with me, or tell me you can't talk or something. Shit. I honestly don't think I've ever sighed into the phone when someone has called me up and asked me out somewhere. This is the second time that has happened to me.

I called Amy back and we fought some more and eventually semi-made up. For now, it seems as if everything is okay.

I don't think I will be calling Andrea. If she wants to call me, she will. And as much as I hate it, I still feel like calling her after the holidays, when things settle down a bit. It's like I'm a battered wife, and as much as I hate it, I can't break away from my husband. I want to engage in behavior that is probably not in my best interest. I won't engage in it, but it sucks that I even want to.

I'm very thankful for having Amy. I'm also happy with her most of the time. It's just that she's the only relationship I've ever had, and the only chick I've ever slid my penis into. I have to know if she truly is the one. If I go out with a few other people, and come back to her, then I will have more faith in our relationship. If I choose someone else, either I'm making a huge mistake or I've really found someone I like more, or maybe even a little of both. I don't want to marry the wrong woman, and I certainly don't want to have kids with someone from whom I will grow apart.

Hell, I don't even want to have kids. I just want to make the right choices and have a happy life. There are better things to worry about than money and choosing the right marriage partner. Not that those aren't valid things to worry about or fight over, it's just that I'd rather spend my time not worrying about those things so I can concentrate on what's really important. I'd rather set my life up to where I don't have to worry about money, or marriage, so when I do worry about something related to either of those things, it actually counts for something. I don't know if I'm making sense here, but to me it's perfectly clear.

It's perfectly okay to doubt what you have, but don't do it to the point where it hurts your relationship. Think about how good you have it, not how good you could have it. If Andrea does eventually give me a chance, will I really be happier? Probably not. There is a balance. Don't limit yourself to just one person too early on, yet don't discount that one person at all, even with what you perceive to be their faults. Their faults make them who they are just as much as their assets.

Andrea's sigh helped me realize that I do have something meaningful that I really don't want to lose. Her sigh made me realize what it would be like to be single, trying to ask women out and going through the games we all play when we're dating.

But more importantly, Andrea's sigh made me realize that I probably wasn't going to get any pussy off of her, so I should not waste any more of my time. I should devote my time to the only source of pussy I have—Amy.

CHAPTER 7

The Lawnmower Man

(A friend of mine who used to publish women's books looked over a few chapters of this book and commented that Andrea didn't deserve two chapters. She's right; Andrea doesn't deserve mention in this piece of literature. However, I wrote the following for this book and am keeping it in so you can read it. Think of it as the equivalent of a deleted scene on a DVD.)

Of all the classrooms in all the buildings in all the campuses in all the world, I had to go walking into hers.

And what an astronomical coincidence it was, too. My school has an enrollment of about 20,000 people. I am one of them. Of the remaining 19,999 people, she is one of them. That leaves 19,998 people. The average class is probably made up of 45 people, given the fact that many lecture courses have between 150-200 people enrolled. There are more small classes than there are big ones, so I base my estimate at 45 people considering that a few big classes can bring that number up.

19,998 divided by 45 equals about 444. The chances of me being in a class with her are 1 in 444 at the outset, regardless of anything else.

Now, I could make this a lot more complex considering the number of classes available, when they're available, major, etc. but there is no reason. I just want to point out that the odds of this happening are amazing.

Especially considering the fact that I didn't even want to take the class in the first place. I was finishing up my general education credits so I could graduate, and I needed one more science class. Someone recommended that I take my last science from a biology teacher who was retiring. He didn't give a shit what anyone did. It was basically an easy class. Students wouldn't even be required to buy the $80 biology book! Pretty sweet.

I show up for the first day of biology class, and the administrators changed the class that the soon-to-be retiree was teaching, and guess what, he wasn't teaching mine. I raced to try to add the new class, but it was closed. I asked him to add me to his class, and he wouldn't. That was the first time a teacher wouldn't add me to their filled class.

Fuck.

What science can I take? I never had chemistry in high school, so college chemistry seemed daunting. I didn't want biology, as I know it can be hard (especially at my school). I had already taken natural science, so I was stuck between geography and geology, two subjects which don't interest me in the least.

I grudgingly chose geography. Now, I had to find a lab. Lab courses are separate from the main course, yet they still both have to be taken in order to fulfill my general education requirement.

The labs were all full. They might as well have been, anyway. Every single open lab conflicted with another class. It was clear that I was going to have to change my lab to an inconvenient one, which would screw with my work schedule.

I chose one on Friday. I had no other classes on Friday, and hadn't gone to school on Friday in over two years. This sucked. I kept checking the schedule during the week we could still add courses, though, and every other lab was closed.

Then, suddenly, in the last hour of being able to add a class, a much more convenient one opened up! I crossed my fingers, dropped the lab I was in, and enrolled in the lab that had just one chair open. This was a much better lab, as it was in the middle of the week. I had to get it . . . c'mon . . . YES! I am enrolled in a convenient lab. No school on Friday!

I go to lab, and oh my god, this class is demeaning. I've never learned more common sense stuff in my life. After an hour-and-a-half, the teacher dismisses us. As I'm putting on my book bag, I look down to see a face looking at me.

It's her.

The bitch that completely used me.

Her.

The bitch that has four of my phone numbers, yet only called when she needed help, and hasn't called since.

It was Andrea.

Not two fucking weeks after writing about her for this book, I saw her again. Not because I chose to, and certainly not because she chose to, but rather, because of astronomical odds. Had the biology teacher's schedule not changed, I would not be in this class. Had someone not dropped out of this geography lab at the very last minute, I would not be looking at her at this very moment. She was practically sitting right in front of me for 90 minutes and I never even knew it.

We made small talk while walking towards our cars. She's taking 19 hours to graduate this semester, and working 40 hours a week. I gotta say that this is the only part of her life that I truly respect. That's hard to do.

I was so stunned at seeing her again, that I forgot the magic words. Sure, I told her about how I just received two raises, and how it's all downhill for me, oh, and that I just came back from a trip to Las Vegas where I stayed in a hotel room with a Jacuzzi, yet I forgot the fucking magic words. I wish I could go back in time to say them, so I know what she would have done. Those words . . .

YOU OWE ME LUNCH.

I forgot all about that until pulling into my driveway at home.

At first, I thought being in the same lab with Andrea was a blessing. And in a way it probably is. It teaches me more about why chicks suck, and why she's not even worthy of being written about.

The very next week, she literally ignored me. I got to class first, and had an empty seat next to me. When she walked in, she just sat in the first empty seat she found.

I was offended. The only thing I remembered about the class was that she was in it. I didn't know the instructor's name, or even exactly what time the class began. I did remember that she was the one I knew in the class. I didn't really want to know anyone else in the class, as it was an embarrassment that I even had to take it. A third-grader could have passed this course with flying colors, and many in the class struggled with some of the most elementary concepts, such as time zones. The class consisted of many white jocks, white trash, and black jocks. Not exactly the type of people I like to hang with.

So, instead of sitting next to someone I at least knew, I sat next to an empty seat, with no one to talk to, learning material that I already knew. Even though the class was only an hour long, it seemed to last three. Finally, the graduate student dismissed us, and Andrea left without even looking at me.

Now, I understand that people have many things on their minds. She may have been in a rush (she wasn't) or maybe she had her period and had to change a tampon or something (she didn't). So, I tried not to let it bother me.

But it did bother me. A lot. Let's take the issue of sex and gender out of this. If Andrea were a guy, and I had helped her/him on a final when I didn't even have to, then I would expect some gratitude. And if I were in a class with a guy who I had studied with, chances are I would at least acknowledge his presence, if he didn't acknowledge mine first. And maybe the guy would at least suck my cock, which Andrea definitely should have done.

So, I thought I'd ignore the bitch the next week, and that's exactly what I did. I arrived in class after she did, and we happened to be taking a test in the class that day. So, instead of ripping through the test like I usually do, I stalled just a bit and timed it so I left class just a tad earlier than her, instead of much earlier. Once I realized she was behind me, I acted like I was in a huge rush, and walked as fast as I could to my car, and I didn't look back once. I wasn't running, but I was walking pretty damn fast.

There is a street between the parking lot and the school. So, once I arrived at the street I had to stop. When I looked to my left to see oncoming cars, I saw her out of the corner of my eye, she was not more than six feet away from me. Wow, she must have been walking really fast to catch up with me, or maybe she was actually in a hurry (doubt it). I got across the street as fast as I could and drove to work, ignoring her the whole time. If the grass is always greener on the other side of the fence, then I became the lawnmower man.

In retrospect, I'd like to think that because we got out of class so early that she was trying to catch up with me to ask me to lunch (she wasn't). If she had actually done that, I don't know if I would have said yes, as I would have told her that I was in a hurry and taken a rain check. Ya know, play the game with her. Or even better, I could have told her that I was meeting my girlfriend Amy for lunch. She would have both despised me and wanted me at the same time if I had done that.

But I did feel better about ignoring her. Ever hear of a white lie? I thought of it as a white revenge, if that makes sense. I didn't really hurt anyone by ignoring her.

Some of you may think that my actions are akin to acting like the assholes and jerks I complain about on my Web site. I can see how someone might think that, but that's absolutely not the case. Sure, a trick many guys have told me to do is to ignore a chick. That's the best way to get laid, because as soon as you communicate to a chick that you don't want her, that makes you a challenge, and she must prove to herself that she could get you if she wanted. I can admit that I wanted to test that theory a bit with Andrea.

However, the fact remains that if Andrea was a guy, and I helped him out studying, and we seemed to hit it off as friends, yet afterwards he didn't need me and he never called me and then ignored me in a class we had together, I'd be pissed off, and I'd ignore him. The fact that Andrea was a chick just meant that I might get laid if I ignored her. Of course, it can be argued that if Andrea were a guy, I'd have never helped her out in the first place, which is not the case. I've studied with plenty of guys. In fact, I regularly hung out with a guy from the class Andrea and I met in—after I helped him out on the last two tests in the class. And for the record, he never gave me a blowjob, but he didn't ignore me either.

We didn't have class the week after that, as my school was on Spring Break that week. The week after that, though, we did have class. I was like a minute late, and when I came in I sat down next to that empty chair, the same empty chair I sat next to when I first started attending that class. Andrea didn't have a seat next to her, but if she had I would not have sat next to her anyway. After class, I had to walk by her to get out of the room. I made a fatal mistake—I made eye contact. Shit, I had to say something. I kept walking, but I said, "Hey," in a friendly tone. Her response? A blank stare to my right, as if she was looking at someone standing behind me.

Ok, bitch. I'll never speak to you again, if that's what you'd like. The building in which we have class is oddly shaped, and it's in a weird location. I was out of the building first, but I went the long way around. When I turned a corner, she was there, and I was in her full view, and she completely ignored me.

I think it's obvious that this is a case of two people who are pissed off at each other for various reasons. The fact is that while our class is supposed to be dismissed at 1:00pm, we routinely get out before noon. She has a class at 1:00, and I try to be at work by 1:30 at the latest. So, why on earth would she ever be in so much of a hurry that she couldn't even say two words to me, especially as she had about 90 minutes to make it to her next class?

If I cared enough, I'd call her. I have two of her phone numbers. I'd like to ask her what her deal is, if she treats everyone who bends over backwards to help her like she has treated me. Or if she lets out long audible sighs whenever someone asks for a lunch that she said she'd give them. But I don't care enough. I care enough to share the experience with all of you, as it fills up pages in this book and makes it longer, but I do not care to confront her on this shit, as I do not believe that anything good will come out of it for either of us. Since nothing good can happen, I see no point in confrontation.

One real shame is that she physically turns me on. I don't even know why. Most guys probably would only think she's a 6 or a 7 on a 1-10 scale. But something about her just really gets the juices of my loins flowing. I was masturbating to a porno flick this morning, and for a second, I thought of her. I don't know why, but I did, and it turned me on. I could have turned off that porn and masturbated to my thoughts of how attractive she was and finished quite easily. Of course, I didn't, as I wouldn't want to give her the satisfaction that she can get me off without even being there. Even if she didn't know, in a strange way I'd feel like I'd be submitting to her. That of course, would be wrong.

I've actually been writing this chapter throughout the whole semester, sporadically updating it after some of these classes. I get angry and depressed that I am reminded of my failure every time I see her. No, that's not it. Rather, I get angry that I let myself be used so willingly. I am angry with her, too, though. I'm angry that she can easily use me and pretend that I don't exist.

The class met for the last time today. The very last time. That means that I've seen Andrea for the last time, since I'm graduating. I was looking over some handouts in preparation for the final, and I looked up and she came in, wearing a black leather jacket and a purple halter top—the same one she was wearing when I was staring down her shirt the previous semester. Her tits were huge, but her hair wasn't washed. After about the fourth or fifth class, she stopped washing her hair in the morning, and she wasn't quite as attractive to me. But her body just drove me wild, and it still does.

And I guess that is another reason I'm angry. I'm still physically attracted to her, big time. When people piss me off, I usually hold a grudge for a long time. Once someone earns my trust and betrays it, they've lost me in their life forever.

Did Andrea betray my trust? In a way. Sure, I helped her out of the goodness of my heart, but in helping her, my goal obviously was not to have her ignore me the rest of her life. At the very least I would have loved to make another friend. None of that happened, and that was her choice. Fine, but at least be honest with me. Don't fucking use me.

Am I wrong for writing about her when she doesn't know it? Absolutely not. If she can use me, I feel that I can use her for material.

Andrea joins a very select group of people. There are very few women that completely knock the wind out of me before they say a word. She was one of them. I don't like supermodels or Barbie dolls, no, I'm attracted to real people, and yes, that includes people with physical imperfections (and Andrea did have a few, most notably her skin on her ring and index fingers of her left hand were pigmented differently from the rest of her olive-colored skin.)

The odds of all of this happening are quite amazing, though. If Andrea and I had actually gotten together, we could say that it was meant to be, that fate intervened in both of our lives, that God made us for each other, that we would know a love almost unimaginable by human beings.

That didn't happen, so I don't know what to say, except that if there is a God, She must really fucking hate me.

CHAPTER 8

Andrea Analysis

I did quite a few things wrong with Andrea. I also did quite a few things right.

One of the biggest things I did wrong is that I planned ahead. My time is extremely valuable to me, but I am not so structured in how I spend my time that I'm anal about it. I can be spontaneous and do something without planning, however I have to admit that I do make plans and generally stick with them.

The mistake I made with Andrea was that I counted on her to conform to my plans. For instance, when I got an extra review sheet from my teacher to give to her, I was planning on seeing her to give it to her. I made plans for her to come by my job and pick it up, and then I planned for us to go to lunch.

That's fine. That's not the mistake. The mistake is not having a backup plan.

Who did I go to lunch with that day? Nobody, because Andrea didn't call me until everyone else had gone to lunch. I ate alone that day, and I don't like eating alone.

What I did right was coming up with the plans. For instance, if she had stopped by my work, I would have nonchalantly brought up going to lunch. It would have seemed like a spontaneous idea; at least I would have brought it up like one. Even if she turned me down, I was at least strategizing. But the real mistake was counting on her to say yes. I needed a plan B. "If she doesn't call me by 12:30, I'm going to go to lunch with the marketing guys."

Helping her on her test was a bad move. A little help would have been fine, but I almost literally bent over backwards for her, going to work late so I could help her out. Bad, bad move.

I think noticing her sigh after I asked her out, replying, "You don't sound too excited about *that*." That was not a mistake. I stood up for myself. My mistake was not bringing it up again, and not saying, "So, do you sigh when other people who have shown you nothing but kindness ask you out on a date, or just me?" God knows I was angry enough to say that.

Definitely, forgetting the fact she owed me lunch when I saw her again—that was a mistake.

And if I send her a copy of this book, I think that'd be a *huge* mistake.

CHAPTER 9

The Internet Is Evil

I love New York City. I went for the first time about a year ago and took Amy with me. We both really wanted to check out Central Park, so we hopped on the subway and went to Manhattan.

We went to the Metropolitan Museum of Art and spent about two hours there. Outside of the museum there are some small outdoor tourist traps, selling everything from beads to pictures of NYC landmarks.

I figured that the temperature in New York during April would be cool. That day it turned out to be like 90 degrees. I was wearing a nice dress shirt, and it was so hot that I decided to let Amy look at the tourist trap stuff. I told her I was going to sit down on one of the many benches around.

I found an empty bench and sat down, admiring the city. I was looking at the endless stream of people walking by when an Asian girl sits next to me.

"Do you have the time?" she asks.

"3:05," I replied, noticing that she was wearing a watch.

"Are you John?"

"No."

"Oh, I'm sorry. I'm supposed to meet someone here. Have you ever done the Internet dating?"

So that's what was going on. This girl was talking to me because I was dressed nicely and she was probably hoping that I was John. I looked around and noticed a few other guys by themselves, but she came to me because I was dressed nicely.

I took a second look at her and she wasn't bad looking at all. I have a thing for Asian chicks anyway, like most white guys my age. She was thin, looked pretty intelligent, and was really easy to talk to.

Amy looked over and saw that I was macking on an Asian chick. She smiled at me.

The Asian chick was awaiting my response.

"No," I said. I was lying, though.

When I first got online in 1995, I immediately saw the Internet's greatest use—porn. A friend of mine came over and I showed him how to get porn from IRC. He said, "I am never leaving your house. I can't believe it. It's like there is nothing at all that you can't find."

He then asked if anyone in the room (#sexpics) had a picture of a woman and a fish. Seconds later, !fishfuc.jpg was on its way. While the picture was blurry, and the fish could have been a prop, there was no doubt at all about what one could find on the Internet.

After a while, I started learning how to use the Internet to meet women. I was having little luck offline, and the Internet was so new to the mainstream that not even Internet stalkers had been invented yet.

When I worked at the software store in the mall, one of the perks was having a free Prodigy account for 20 hours a month. I already had free Internet access through my school, but sometimes the lines were busy, so Prodigy was a good backup.

One day I'm home from school, and I get on Prodigy. Somehow I meet a girl who claims to be in Seattle. She tells me she's a lingerie model. When I ask to see her picture she gets a little perturbed and says that's the first thing everyone asks her after she says that. Well, fucking duh! If I told you that I have three dicks, you'd probably want to see some proof.

Over the chat rooms we hit it off. We eventually called each other and she had a great sounding voice. She told me she modeled for Frederick's of Hollywood.

I knew there was a possibility she could be lying, but shit, I wanted to believe her so badly. I found out a lot about her, like how she was caught by a cop when she and her friends were skinny-dipping, and the cop was an asshole about it and made them all get out of the water nude.

I never did get her to send me her picture, but she did tell me that I should guess which model was her. So, I stopped by my local Frederick's store to pick up a catalog. A friend of mine with a scanner let me scan in who I thought she was. I sent her the scan, telling her my guess, and she replied that I was correct.

She moved and we eventually lost touch. Actually, she lost touch with me.

If I was correct about which model she was, though, then I hit the fucking mother lode, because that girl turned out to be Brooke Burke from the E! Network's *Wild On!* series. However, Brooke's real name must also be Patricia and her voice must have changed since we last talked in 1996. While Brooke looked hot in *Playboy*, I somehow doubt that I met her on a chat room in Prodigy, although I absolutely would love it if it turned out to be true. Have I mentioned that I have three dicks?

Having been burned from the girl in Seattle, I figured I should set my sites a little more local. I figured out how to tell if people online were local or not, and started going to local-themed chat rooms and meeting people there. Shit, *I* probably was the first Internet stalker.

If I remember correctly, the very first chick I met was pure white trash. She had told me she was 40 or something, so I started making fun of her for being old. I cracked old jokes left and right and she told me that she was going to have to meet me. I drove forever to her house, because she lived in the fucking boonies, and I don't know why I met her, but I did. I guess I was bored. She had like 3 children, was a chain smoker, but she was physically attractive for her age, if you can overlook the fact that she was a hillbilly.

I thought what happened next was extremely weird. We were talking a little bit, and I was still making fun of her for being old, and then she got online and went to a chat room and started talking to people. I would like to say she was ignoring me, but she wasn't. She was pointing to people's screen names saying things like, "That there is Billy-Bob. He lost both legs in the war."

After about five minutes of that, I bid her adieu, and never spoke with her again.

A few months later, I met a girl on IRC who happened to be a student at my school. We met in person, and she was just an average girl. I guess she sort of liked me, as she invited me to go to a local music festival with her. She was from out of town and didn't really know anyone, and we got along okay.

We went to the concert, and she wound up hooking up with some guy near us. Crowds aren't my scene at all, but I noticed that within like 10 minutes he had his arms around her and she was leaning back on him. I had a lot to learn about being smooth with women, as I never would have even attempted to touch this girl like that, especially after only a few minutes of knowing her. She moved away and I lost touch with her.

Another chick I met lived about five minutes away from me. She lived with her brother and the very night we met she wanted me to come by her place. I did. She liked me as a friend, but I wasn't going to get anywhere with her. She did show me some topless photos of herself, though.

I kept in touch with this chick, until she got carjacked. She then dropped out of school and told me she was moving away. "Your whole perspective on life changes after you've had a double-barrel shotgun shoved in your face," she told me. I not only lost touch with her, but I probably lost an outlet to meet other people, as this girl was definitely my friend.

I chatted with another chick on AOL who lived about an hour away. She liked me. She sent me pictures. She was very tall and looked like a nice person. Two weeks later, she said she had a dream that I was hiding something from her, and she said that if I didn't tell her what it was, then that's the same as lying to her. I told her that was the most ridiculous thing I've ever heard, and that I wasn't hiding anything from her (kind of hard to hide anything from anyone when you've never met them). I never heard from her again.

One of the worst experiences involved yet another girl who went to my school. We started emailing each other and I talked to her on the phone, and she sounded nice enough. We met on campus and my God she was huge! I'm a bigger person but she could have easily swallowed two of me. She had to weigh about 350-400 pounds, no joke. If I'm wrong, it's even more.

But I tried to have an open mind. She asked if we could pick up a friend of hers and I said sure. She was driving. We picked up her friend who was apparently her twin sister, because her friend weighed as much as she did!

Again, I'm trying to be positive about everything. Her friend gets in the front passenger's seat, and she's driving, so that leaves me in the back seat. We were trying to figure out something to do, so we drove around the city for about an hour, during which time they talked to each other, completely ignoring me. Now, I was mad. It's bad enough that I'm hanging out with two chicks who were so fat that their stretch marks had stretch marks, but they have the gall to pretend I'm not even there? Knowing that honesty would get me dumped on the side of the road, I quickly made up an excuse as to why I had to be driven to my car immediately. I think I told them that I missed my trough-feeding time. I'm sure they hate it when that happens to them, so I figured they'd buy that excuse.

They did, and I don't believe I ever talked to that chick again. I saw her once or twice on campus, and she completely ignored me. That was fine with me.

Another chick I met was hot but a complete dullard. She didn't like me at all and was probably just as boring with people she did like, but God I wanted to get down her pants.

One chick I met on IRC who also happened to go to my school was yet another out-of-towner. Her name was Gina. I don't remember where she was from, but I do remember that we talked on the phone within a few times of us chatting online. She was pretty liberal as far as politics went, and she was in law school. She was also older than I was, by two or three years.

After a few nights, she tried to initiate phone sex with me. As I've said on the site, I did not masturbate until I was 19 years old. And I wish I could go back in time and fix that, but I cannot. Gina was trying to initiate phone sex, and I kept telling her that I did not masturbate. She already knew I was a virgin at that time. I can't imagine what must have been going through her head as she was saying things like, "Just touch yourself and start rubbing up and down," when I replied, "No, really, I can't." No wonder I couldn't get laid.

For some reason we didn't talk for a few months, but when I saw her online again and chatted with her, she suggested that we meet on campus. I said sure. She was supposed to get there at 9:00pm. I waited around until 9:15 and figured I'd been fucked with when a girl comes up to me and asks if I'm me. She tells me that she's Gina. She's gotten pretty dressed up, and she smells nice. She was a little over-weight, but not really fat. She had blonde hair and some nice cans.

She suggests I drive her somewhere. I ask her where, and she says we'll figure it out when we get into the car.

So I start driving and I'm just casually talking to her, much the same way I'm talking to you right now, when she takes my hand off of the armrest and puts it on her left tit. I look at her and she's giving me "the look." I knew I was going to score.

As we passed by a Wendy's, she said she was thirsty and asked if I would buy her a Dr. Pepper. I said sure.

I'm driving along towards the suburbs and we find an abandoned lot where I'm sure someone's house now stands. I shut off my car and she asks me to get out of the car while she does something. I asked her what she was going to do, and she wouldn't tell me. I took my keys out of the ignition, put them in my pocket and stepped outside[4].

After about a minute she opens the car door and I start grabbing her tits and fingering her. We go into the back seat and she unzips my pants and grabs my cock. Instantly I shoot off. This is the first time I've ever been this far with a woman, and it didn't even feel good. It was like, now I'm dry, now she touches me, now I'm wet. No orgasm. Nothing. Pissing felt better. At least pissing lasts longer than 2 seconds.

I proceeded to eat her out for at least an hour, possibly even two. I sucked her tits, ate her pussy and gave her a great time, while I wasn't having much fun at all. However, I was finally getting some, and I was thankful, even though I was the one doing all the work. Hell, that didn't even bother me, as I had always fantasized about eating pussy. That and doggy-style were always two things I wanted to try.

One weird thing, though, was that when she took off her panties, she said that she had a scar on her anus that came from a childhood

[4] It literally just occurred to me why she asked me to do this. I think she was putting in a diaphragm or spermicide. Keep this in mind. It comes into play later.

accident, or something akin to that. Now, it's pretty much pitch black. There's no way possible I would notice a scar. If she hadn't told me, I'dve never known. I mean, what the Hell was I going to do, even if I could see her anus? Say, "OH MY GOD! WHAT HAPPENED TO YOUR ANUS?!" It's not like my nose was in her anus or anything. I had a hard enough time seeing her pussy, and she knew that. Why even bring your anus up?

Eventually, this chick wants to get kinkier. I'm taking a breather, as I'm fucking beat. I've been eating this girl out for quite a while now and it has taken its toll on me. As I'm catching my breath, she asks me for the Dr. Pepper. I give it to her. She takes the straw, puts her finger over one end, takes it out of the cup, and removes her finger from the straw, pouring the Dr. Pepper on her pussy. She then asks me to eat her out some more.

I was a fucking virgin. You don't send a new firefighter into a blazing building; you train him first. She was a five-alarm fire. I told her that I was really beat and needed to catch my breath, and she started masturbating. I eventually got on top of her again and started kissing her tits. She had told me that she did not want me to penetrate her with my dick, and I didn't have any condoms anyway, as I was not expecting to get any action at all. As I was kissing her tits, I nudged my dick near her pussy and she said, "Don't fuck me."

And I didn't.

I eventually took her back to campus.

I went home and started to think about what had just happened. I was not ashamed of myself, but I can't say that I enjoyed myself either. So why didn't I enjoy it? I didn't like the Dr. Pepper thing at all, and I didn't like that I had shot off so fast. I thought there could be something wrong with me.

Then I thought about what I wanted to do if I had the opportunity again, and I wanted more foreplay. More kissing, for sure. That would have gotten me hotter.

The next night she called me up and asked me if I wanted to go out. Sure, I said. She also said that when she told me to not fuck her when I was on top of her, she really wanted me to fuck her hard. I didn't have a condom, so that wasn't going to happen, but I found that pretty odd. Maybe that's why she was putting the diaphragm in? Who knows.

So we met at the same place, hopped in my car, and went behind a grocery store near my house. We got into the back seat and I started kissing her passionately.

"I don't like to kiss," she said.

I was shocked, but I was going to get some more play, so I didn't say anything. She got on top of me and rubbed her pussy up and down my chest. I did not enjoy that at all. I was not having fun. I lived with my parents. She had roommates. We were fucking behind a grocery store in my car. It was cramped. I wasn't getting to do the things I wanted to do.

We got our clothes on and I started driving back to campus. I started to talk to her but she wasn't saying anything. I stopped talking. Dead silence in the car for about five minutes.

I started thinking to myself, "How am I going to blow this girl off? Do I just tell her that I'm not having fun with her? I really want to be friends with her, but I now know for sure that there's nothing wrong with me—I'm just not getting what I want out of this."

When she had called me that night she had talked about having a threesome with one of my male friends. This girl was pretty kinky, that's for sure. I just know none of my friends would have been into that sort of thing. I never told her what I wanted, though. I just wanted to get laid, or at least get some experience. I was too inexperienced to even think about what I wanted. I knew I wanted to kiss, though, and I got rejected on that one. She also told me that when I was kissing her tits and I had nudged my cock near her pussy and she told me not to fuck her, that she really wanted me to. Fucked up. This was my first time with a chick ever and I'm supposed to know to do the opposite of what she says?!

So, we're sitting in total silence until I pull up to her car in the campus parking lot. She opens my car door and says, "Don't contact me again."

"Ok," I said, feeling some relief.

She had left her bra in my car, and I said, "You forgot this," handed her the bra, and drove off.

A few days later, I'm on IRC and I see her there. I say hi to her and she says, "Want some more?"

I replied, "Actually, no I don't. I don't think we're sexually compatible at all. I'd still like to be your friend though."

I meant it, but she was incensed. I had just rejected her, and she was not happy at all. I never spoke to her again.

The Internet finally got me some action, but even the previous story can't compare to the granddaddy of them all.

I'm on Yahoo! personals[5], probably doing research for this book, and I see a chick's ad in my area. She says she wants to fuck. I contact her on Yahoo! Instant Messenger, make some small talk, then ask her if she wants to fuck. She says sure. She said I'd have to go to her place, though, and she lived with her family. I said no way, that she'd have to meet me and we'd go to a hotel.

So, I meet her and like the idiot that I am, forgot to bring the condoms. This girl is short and thin, but has a shapely body. Just an average girl, really, nothing remarkable about her, but she is, as the French would say, *très* doable.

We went to buy condoms, and then to the hotel. The clerk said that there was a chance that the maid hadn't been by yet, but I figured how bad could it be?

We get to the room and it smelled like damp towels had been sitting out in the open, and that's because they had been! I apologized to her, but figured we wouldn't be using the room long. I undressed to my boxers and she started giving me shit about not wanting me to see her naked or something. I talked her out of that, telling her she was pretty and I got her out of her shirt and pants. She covered her body, though; her face with one hand, her tits with the other arm. I started kissing her all over and she was wearing these neon green panties and I could see that they were wet. But she wouldn't let me see her body.

"Relax," I said, and I proceeded to give her oral through the panties. I finally got them off of her and asked her to turn around so I could see her ass. She wouldn't. And she kept her face covered the entire time.

---

[5] http://personals.yahoo.com

This, as you can imagine, was not the biggest turn on for me. I slipped on a condom and started to fuck her missionary style. I had masturbated a couple of hours earlier, so this was not going to be a quickie. After quite a while, I told her to let me turn her over so we could do some doggie-style, and she said no.

"Well fuck," I thought. "She's doing everything to make me *not* cum. I can't see her face, this room sucks, and this isn't any fun. Fuck this, I'm going to make myself cum."

I started thrusting away at her harder than I ever have to anyone in my life. She said ouch at once point, and when I asked her if I had hurt her, she said no. Well, shit, if she's going to lie to me, I should at least believe her.

After about another five minutes, during which time I am dripping sweat on her because I'm fucking her so hard, I finally cum. Even though I'm wearing a condom, I make sure to pull out before I shoot. I looked down and the condom wasn't on.

Holy fuck.

To this day, I believe it came off as I pulled out of her. I hope so, anyway. I don't have any STDs, so I should be fine. But I had to reach up into her and get the condom, and let me tell you it was WAY up inside her.

I caught my breath and it was time to go. I called Amy and told her I had sex with someone else. At first she didn't believe me, but then she knew I wasn't kidding.

I told Amy that I'd take her to the hotel room and fuck her there. She thought it was a great idea, so she and I went to the hotel. The best part of this was that the female clerk who had checked me in earlier when I was with the other girl was still there! When I walked in with Amy, she gave me a very weird look, one of disgust, yet also of bewilderment. How does a guy that looks like me get two broads in a day?

Amy and I go into the room, which, by the way, smelled exactly the same as when I left it. We fuck. I told Amy that the hotel clerk gave me a weird look, so we should pour it on when we check out. I asked Amy to leave me alone with the clerk.

We go to check out. It's 9 or 10:00pm, and Amy is all smiles. "It was really thoughtful of you to get this hotel room," she says, right in front of the clerk.

"I'm just a thoughtful guy," I replied.

"I love you so much," she said.

"And I love you, and only you," I said.

"I'm going to go out to the car, honey." Amy exits.

The clerk rang me up, and I could tell she just wanted to speak her mind to me, but she didn't. She couldn't, as it was probably against the hotel's policy to bitch at guys who fuck multiple girls in the same day in the same room. She was just itching to say something to me, though. I wish I could know exactly what.

The next day I'm online and I see the girl. I said hi to her and she replied, "A/S/L."[6] Wow, she was a real cum bucket.

I replied, "It's the guy you fucked yesterday," hoping I was indeed the only guy she did fuck yesterday.

The very first response from her is that my dick was small. What a bitch! I give her the ramming of her life and she complains?! If I were any larger, my dick would have come out of her throat!

She then tells me that I raped her, and that I wanted the condom to fall off so she would get pregnant. I was floored. If she was serious about the rape thing, it could really suck for me. Luckily, making the scene in front of the clerk would have really helped my case, as there's no way in hell that the clerk would have forgotten me.

When she told me that I raped her and wanted to get her pregnant, I replied, "Yup. You found me out! That was the plan all along. I'm pretty slick."

She finally got serious and said that she was just looking for someone to love and that I had used her. Gee, I guess that's what happens when you put an ad up saying that you want to fuck and then you meet a guy that tells you he wants to fuck you, and then you meet him and you fuck.

I think she wanted me to get her pregnant so I'd have to stick around or something. She never said anything to me in person accept "yeah," "ouch," "no," and "why?" That was the other thing about this

---

[6] That's "Age/Sex/Location?" for you non-Internet folk.

chick, all she ever said was "Why?" She'd respond to anything I would ask her, "Why?" She didn't even pronounce the word correctly, instead saying "Wah," with absolutely no inflection in her voice indicating that she was even asking a question. There's no way I could ever love her, not without smacking her around, anyway.

I told her that if she wanted someone to love her, she shouldn't be trying to piss them off by claiming that they raped her and trying to hurt them by telling them that their dick was small. She agreed. She told me that we could meet again the next day, and I should sign on tomorrow to figure out when and where. I told her that I'd try to love her, LOLing the entire time.

I never talked to her again.

The Internet has gotten me laid. But I have yet to receive any enjoyable sex from it. I'm a much better communicator through text than through voice, and the 'net levels the playing field a bit. I just wish I could meet some normal girls online, but I do not expect that to ever happen. Maybe it's because no one online is normal.

Or maybe it's because no one offline is normal. Except for the Asian chick on the bench with me in New York City. She seemed pretty damned normal to me.

I lied to the Asian chick because explaining all of the above would have been too time-consuming. We chatted for about 5 minutes and John finally came by. He was much older than me and he seemed to be a manual-labor type of guy. The Asian chick told me goodbye, and I had a feeling that she would have preferred to go out with me. I don't know what happened on their date, but my guess is that they went out and never talked with each other again.

CHAPTER 10

The Comedy Club

Throughout this book I've made many references to doing standup comedy. Comedy is something I've always wanted to do, as most of my idols are comedians. I especially look up to the late Bill Hicks.

Taking the stage is something that takes huge balls to do. Unlike many other types of performing arts, if you blow it in standup, only you will be blamed. The reason I did it is because I thought I might be successful doing it, and besides, chicks dig a guy who can make them laugh, right?

Every Wednesday night is open mike night at the local comedy club. I found out about it after my first time going. I think I was 19 years old.

I wanted to do comedy when I was 14. Even back then I had an act. Not a good one, mind you, but I had one. When I was 14, all my friends had chicks. Me? I had a comedy act.

I still have that hand-written act, and it's absolutely amazing. I didn't remember half the stuff on the piece of paper, but reading it really brought back some memories. Many people have diaries, yet something tells me that half of the people who keep diaries never ever read them.

Anyhow, my act included stuff that was going on in my life when I was 14. I was, like most teens, preoccupied with school and the social atmosphere that goes with it. Unlike most people, though, I had gone to four schools in one year. Damn.

One of those schools was Deer Park High School in Deer Park, Texas. Deer Park is a suburb of Houston, known nationwide as the city with the worst Six Flags theme park around.

Deer Park was typical suburbia times ten. It was a pretty rich suburb, or at least going to the school made me think that. Deer Park's school board must have thought that throwing money at a school would get rid of all the problems like drugs, bullying, and dropouts. I don't know about the latter two, but I can tell you I've never seen a school with a bigger drug problem.

How much money did this school spend annually? Fuck, I'd like to know, because most of it is wasted. They had two campuses, and if you had a class on the north campus when you were on the south campus, no problem, as buses ran at the end of each period. That's right, they employed full-time bus drivers. In math class, every student was issued a Texas Instruments TI-81 graphing calculator. This was at a time when they first hit the market. Every student got one during Algebra II. It amazed me. In Biology, there were enough microscopes for everyone.

As a side note, I rode the bus to school every day. There was this cute-as-hell chick on the bus, and I noticed her and thought, "I'd fuck her." Then she got up to get off (the bus, silly), and she had something weird going on in her legs. It was like she couldn't straighten them. She was perpetually squatting. But she was hot otherwise. If I could go back, I'd try to get down her pants. Not only were most guys probably not hitting on her, but I could also say I fucked a gimp, and how many people can honestly say that, barring Courtney Cox?

I only went to that high school for six weeks. My parents informed the school that we were only there temporarily, and I, in turn, told my teachers. The whole time I was there, in typical suburban school fashion, only one student talked to me. In six weeks. Granted, I saw no reason to make friends as I was moving anyway, but common courtesy was not extended. Shit, it's hard enough going through adolescence. Going through it alone is a bitch.

DPHS had more rules than any other school I had ever been to. Their student handbook had a section on hazing. I didn't even know what hazing was. They also maintained a strict dress code. Guys could not have earrings, facial hair, or anything else that would "disturb the classroom atmosphere."

One day, my French teacher asked me to take a note to the office. I did. I hadn't shaved in like a week, and I had some facial stubble.

The bitch at the office takes the note, and then says that I have to shave or I'll be suspended (no shit!). She told me that there are rules in the student handbook, and that she can give me a razor to shave. The office had razors, presumably in case a student didn't look just right.

"Wait a second," I said, "I'm not allowed to have a mustache?"

"That's correct," she answered.

"Well, why are you allowed to have one then? I'll shave mine if you shave yours, otherwise you can leave me alone. You have no right to tell me what I must do in the bathroom."

She was pretty shocked, and in a juvenile way, replied, "You don't have to do it in the bathroom."

I eventually did shave, just so you know, but I put a hell of a fight into it. They called my mother and told her to come get me, and she did, and I went home for the rest of the day. Then I shaved. It was only six weeks, so I could handle it. Still, what fucking bullshit. We're wondering why teenagers are killing fellow students? It's bullshit like this. Kids have it tough these days, tougher than even I had it, and if you're going to regulate all aspects of my appearance, break my spirit and make me conform in every way possible, then shit, I might as well take a few with me before I go down myself, because I'd probably be doing them a service.

What pissed me off about the whole ordeal were the student workers around when I refused to shave my stubble (and that's what it was—it was not a beard or a moustache). All of them, both chicks and dudes, looked at me as if I had just raped a four-year-old. The look of shock and disgust on their faces . . . how dare someone challenge the status quo? The bitch at the office even said that the student handbook rules are made not only by teachers, but by students as well.

I'm sure most of you haven't laughed once during this chapter. Remember, I was 14. I told you this shit wasn't funny.

When in DPHS, I was enrolled in band. Actually, I was a band geek throughout my four years of high school. It was an easy A, and very little work. DPHS, however, made band a way of life. I don't know why any high school student in the country would want to be a part of it. The schedule was rigorous. Of course, during the summer, they had band camp. Then, Monday through Thursday was marching rehearsal from 5:30-7:30pm, or something like that. It was two hours a day; that I remember for sure. This is after a student has gone through a whole eight-hour day in school, and presumably has homework. Amazing. Friday was a football game, and Saturday was a parade or a competition, which they usually won. They were the best band in which I had ever played.

Well, I wasn't going to march, as I was only going to be there six weeks. What's the fucking point, right? Thankfully, the band directors (there were two of them) agreed with me.

That one person who talked to me the whole time I was there? He was in band. Played the sax. I was eating lunch, and he came over and asked me why I didn't march. I told him my situation, and he replied that it sucked. We'd say hey to each other in the halls and stuff.

On my very last day at DPHS, in 3rd period, all band students were instructed to come down to the auditorium. I knew it would have nothing to do with me, but I joined them anyway. I saw dude and sat next to him. The secondary band director said he had something important to tell the class: That morning, on my very last day of school at DPHS, one of the band's drummers died in a car wreck.

Damn.

The band director then said something that I'm amazed I had forgotten about until I read it again.

"I don't know if we'll have practice today or not," he said, "but I think we will, as that's the way he would have wanted it."

Oh fuck. I was just amazed at the audacity this guy had. Most teenagers have not had the experience of one of their friends dying. I still haven't, and I'm about to turn 24. This band was a pretty tight-knit group, and for him to say that was both extremely hilarious and insensitive at the same time.

Of course I dare not say, "Yeah, and I think he would have wanted you to shove that baton up your ass too," but I think I should have. It was my last day there, after all.

I can tell you if it were me who died, no one would have shed a tear, not even the one guy who was nice enough to treat me like I existed. I would have liked to have seen that speech, though.

"There was a guy in our band, he was new. He played baritone. He died this morning on the way to school. None of you probably even knew him, or his name, or would even recognize him, as I don't think any of you talked to him ever. Ahh, it was his last day anyway. I don't know if we'll practice today or not, but I'll shove this baton up my ass, as that's what he would have wanted."

I'm pleased to note that my standup act has evolved considerably from the time I was 14. I had gone to the local comedy club, and as soon as they said they had open mike, I knew I would do it. I had to. If I was good enough, not only could I entertain people, but I could make some extra dough and meet some new people (i.e. chicks).

I don't know how the headliners stay in stand up. For every Chris Rock, there's an almost-as-talented unknown who lives in his car and travels 40 weeks a year, hawking a T-shirt at the end of his/her show. Although the payoff could be huge, there's no way I could do that for ten years just for a chance on The Tonight Show and *maybe* something more.

I had almost no material. I looked over the stuff I wrote when I was 14, and as you have discovered, it's really not funny. They're good stories, I think, but they weren't funny. I was still motivated though. Comedy Central had sponsored a contest for their *Don't Quit Your Day Job* CD-ROM. It was a game that was supposed to be funny. The contest was simple: Pick a category, record yourself doing 60 seconds of material related to it, and the top ones will get voted on by users, and the one with the most votes gets a trip to LA.

I did it and promptly forgot about the contest. Months went by, and then I get an email saying I was a finalist and they want to send me some software. I didn't even get my friends to vote for me, and was still a finalist. I could do standup, I thought.

The Wednesday I decided to go, I had that one joke I sent Comedy Central (I think I'll save it for my next book), and . . . nothing else. Then, like mad, I started coming up with yucks left and right. Within a half-hour I had seven minutes of material, including a great opening line. I could do this.

I got there, signed up, and was told to sit with the other open mikers, a few of whom knew each other already, and of course, didn't bother to talk to the new guys. Not that the new guys wanted to talk anyway, at least I didn't, as I was going through my act in my head. I hadn't bothered to bring any friends or family, or even tell them about it. If I bombed, no one would know.

Finally, it was my turn. I went on stage, grabbed the mike and said, "I was talking to a gay friend of mine before the show. He asked me what I was doing tonight. I said, 'I'm going down to open mike.' He looked at me and said, 'Who the hell is Mike?'"

I had a killer finishing joke and the crowd loved me. I got off stage and the other open mikers were impressed. After I got off stage, one of the contractors from my day job said, "Hey man, you're funny!" Shit, the one time I go to fucking open mike night, a guy from work sees me and is going to tell everyone. Fuck.

The next week I went and I killed. That crowd was the best crowd I ever had. Exact same material, exact same delivery, but they were just cracking up much more than the crowd from the first week.

The week after that, I went, and the crowd wasn't warming up to me. Somehow, I don't remember how, I got off on a rant about chicks sucking. It was basically material from my page, about how I couldn't get laid to save my life. And when I did get a little action . . . it didn't work out.

"So, I'm with this fat chick, right?" There was a small audience giggle and some chicks really looked shocked. "What? Every guy here has been with a fat chick. Don't look at me like I'm a freak. Anyhow, I'm with this fat chick, and I'm kissing her all over, ya know, actually doing something for *her*, and she says, 'I don't like to kiss.'"

After I pause with a perplexed look on my face, I said, "So you don't like to kiss, huh? WELL I DON'T LIKE TO FUCK FAT CHICKS!"

The place was howling with laughter. I had won them over. They were with me.

"Ya know, you chicks have it good. You can get laid any time you want," I said.

"Hell yeah!" said a woman from the audience.

"Fuck you!" I replied, with perfect timing, and it really seemed as if I was pissed, because I was. Once you wind me up, you can't stop me.

I got off stage, and the crowd was in love with me. I stayed until the end of the show, and as I was leaving, I held the door open for two chicks behind me. One of them turned to me and said, "Your name is <not telling you>, right?"

"Yes," I said.

"I know you," she replied. She was thin and stacked, and had some great hair.

"I apologize, but you don't look familiar to me at all. I never remember names, but I do remember faces, and I don't know you."

"Yes, but I know you," she said.

"OK, you're starting to freak me out."

"My name's Jamie," she said, "and we've talked on the phone before."

She told me her Internet screen name, and shit, I was floored. This chick hadn't talked to me in at least six months, yet she knew me just from those five minutes. It's amazing I've kept my anonymity on Chicks Suck for so long, come to think of it.

I talked to Jamie and her friend, and walked them to her car. I asked her for her phone number, and she didn't give it to me, saying that she was moving next week. (I was too startled at seeing her to comment on that . . . after I bare my soul on stage, she treats me the exact same way I complain about.)

As she was telling me about her moving situation, a guy walking by said, "Check it out! It's the guy who can't get laid!"

I turned around, pointed at Jamie, and replied, "The night's still young."

Jamie didn't show up the next week and I never heard from her again.

I wouldn't get laid for another 10 months.

CHAPTER 11

Why Guys Suck

We all know chicks suck, but many people think saying so is akin to saying that guys don't. Of course, that theory is horseshit. Guys suck just as much as chicks do, and sometimes even more. However, their behavior is more consistent than chicks'. Guys are not hard to figure out, yet some chicks just don't understand them. Or, rather, they pretend that they don't.

The way we raise men in our culture is just ludicrous. Men can't cry. Men must be able to take pain. We must be ready to fight at any time, and we must never be weak. If we are weak, it better not be publicly. Being gay is the absolute worst thing a heterosexual man can be labeled.

We're pretty fucked in the head, too. Adolescent guys are the most inept at dealing with their sexuality. While we've gone out of our way to teach the most mediocre sex education in our schools (i.e. "We can't be too explicit, or parents will complain."), we've completely ignored sex etiquette. In my middle school, girls and guys weren't even allowed to be in the same classroom when Sex Ed was taught. Do school administrators think that if both sexes learn about sex at the same time in the same room that we'll start dry humping in the classroom? Actually, that would be a disgrace. Dry humping is nothing compared to oral sex.

Males and females need to learn about sex together. What kind of message does separating them send? We need to know what makes the other gender tick. I still really don't know what a pap smear is, although I kind of know. I certainly know it's not a pleasant thing. I had no clue women got cramps until I was a senior in high school. I knew that they got their periods, but had no clue that many chicks get intense pain a few days before their monthly friend visits. I probably didn't even realize that women didn't crap from their vaginas, but I don't know that for sure. I don't know exactly what I knew then. I knew a diaphragm was a form of birth control, but I didn't know until a few weeks ago exactly how it worked.

Since I'm not a chick, I have no idea what you were not taught about us. I'm pretty sure you weren't taught a thing about sex etiquette either. Hell, you were probably given the same pep talk, "When a man and woman love each other . . ."

That's screwed up. That's idealistic and it's just plain wrong. We don't teach our kids that praying before a test will make them get a better grade on it. We do tell them that studying and preparing for a test is their best bet. We don't tell them that pulling out is a surefire method of not getting pregnant. Yet, we'll tell them that sex occurs when two people care about each other very much.

As a culture, we are fucked up about sex. Sex is seen as a negative thing to teach children; hence the separation of the sexes while it's being taught. Sex in the mainstream media (primetime television) is even worse, but it's sure talked about much more so in sitcoms now then when I was a kid. I think that's a good thing, as maybe the teenagers who watch that bullshit will see that sex and love don't necessarily go hand in hand, or even penis in vagina.

But we are screwed up about sex. For instance, most children know that calling a male classmate gay is an insult. Many of those same children don't even know what being gay means. They have no clue about being "out," the stigma it carries, or having to live a secret life if they choose to not be "out." I'm not gay myself; I'm just saying that what two or more consenting adults do behind closed doors is really none of my concern, unless they play their Barbara Streisand music so loud that it shakes the apartment I live in. Otherwise, I've got better things to worry about.

My family and I used to live in a two-story apartment. The television in the living room could be seen from the stairs. My parents and my sister were watching some R-rated flick on cable, and there was a sex scene. I was about 11 years old at the time, and I happened to be on the stairs at that very moment. I could see some guy rubbing all over a girl's tits, kissing her all over. I heard my mom say to my sister, "You're not the one I worry about seeing this. It's your brother I don't want watching this."

Well, why the fuck not?! I was in 7th grade! I had been through Sex Ed, thank you very much. What the hell would be so bad about me watching two people fucking, especially on cable when it's almost always softcore? The most I probably would have seen is some guy's hairy ass bobbing up and down, with the occasional titty thrown in just for kicks.

Seriously, if I saw that, does my mom think that I'd just whip it out in front of my whole family and asked who wanted to play a game of fireman with me as the hose? I mean, how bad is it for me to see a natural human function? I could shit, I could piss, and I was probably able to have sex at that time[7]. Why is it so wrong for me to see someone else doing any of those things if that's what I wanted to see?

Even more fucked up is that it's perfectly acceptable to show the same exact shit on The Discovery Channel or PBS, instead of it being humans, it's like lions or something, and there's no cheesy music. Other than that, though, it's fucking. It's just fine for me to watch two cheetahs doing it, but I can't watch two fellow humans do it?

Those are the same channels that show tribes in Africa and South America and shit, and their women don't wear tops and the guys where the tribal version of Western thong bikini bottoms. They can show all the male ass and female tits they want on PBS, under the guise of it being educational, yet they can't show a naked female body to male students, or a naked male body to female students for educational purposes, unless it was sculpted in stone 2000 years ago.

Now, I realize that young guys are a little more immature when it comes to sex than young chicks are. In my seventh-grade health class, our teacher asked us to take a piece of paper and write whether we were male or female on it. Underneath that, she wanted us to write one or two words that sex means to us. Since we didn't have to write our names on the paper, we could be as honest as we wanted. Most chicks in the class put "reproduction" or "having babies." How lame! The

---

[7] I probably could have done all three of those things at once.

number one response from the guys was "fun." One friend of mine wrote "pussy."

Even in seventh grade, chicks and guys are vastly different. Just a few years after that, either most of the girls realized how stupid an answer "reproduction" was and started having sex for fun, or they had actually used sex to reproduce.

Back to the point, though, if instructors did show a picture or two of a naked woman to boys during Sex Ed, many of them would be laughing or cheering. Well, what's wrong with that? You'd finally have students excited about learning! When else would you complain that the students were too interested in the course material? What, they're supposed to take it seriously? As long as they learn about preventing pregnancy and safe sex, a few hoots and giggles are a far cry from a few single mommies. Furthermore, there would probably be less hooting and giggling if our society were more open about sex to our young people.

We even have to have permission slips for Sex Ed. If your parents didn't sign the slip, you couldn't learn more about being a human being. Funny, I could learn about all the wars, religious crusades, and even play games like dodge ball or football where it wouldn't be hard to break a leg, yet if someone wanted to teach me why my penis sometimes gets hard and makes me feel good, I'm not allowed to learn why without my parents knowing? Huh? I always felt sorry for that one kid whose parents didn't sign that slip. I just think that's the same thing as a kid whose dad is in the KKK telling the school, "I don't want my kid to read no books written by no niggers."

Amy knew a girl in high school. This girl couldn't get pregnant. She was sterile. Sterile Girl actually told her friends that pulling out always did the trick. According to Sterile Girl, you couldn't get pregnant if your man pulled out. Her friends were mostly ignorant Baptists. (Yes, I know, a redundancy.)

Guess what happened? One of her friends (incidentally not a Baptist) believed her. She got with a guy, he pulled out, and her egg was fertilized. I believe she was 16 or 17 years old. All because she was sheltered and uneducated (and so was the guy, who was Baptist, for the record), no one had ever been allowed to be explicit and frank with them and treat them as human beings. Instead, they were treated like children, not like human beings who had a right to know about their own bodies, and because of that this ignorant girl was now pregnant. She gave the kid up for adoption. While I'm sure she regrets the decision, at least it did society some good. There aren't enough white babies up for adoption these days.

This next story comes from a friend of mine who also knew Sterile Chick. Sterile Chick and my friend's roommate had gotten together and started doing the horizontal mombo. You know, porking each other. I know this because my friend walked in on them. Here's the clincher: His roommate wanted to become a Baptist preacher! How hysterical is that?!

Well, one day, one of Sterile Chick's friends called and asked for Baptist Preacher Wannabe Who Is A Devout Christian But Loves To Fuck Outside Marriage. Baptist Preacher Wannabe wasn't in, but my friend knew this girl pretty well, or at least well enough to ask her a question. This is all hearsay, but I believe it, as my friend wasn't nearly smart enough to make this shit up.

He asked her how Baptist Preacher Wannabe could truly be a devout Christian if he's fucking outside of marriage. She said, "There are ways."

"How?" my friend asked.

"Oh, you know . . ." she said.

"No, I don't know! Please, tell me how!"

My friend said there was a slight pause.

"Well, you know how girls have a cherry?" the girl asked.

"Yes," my friend replied, confused, yet with extreme curiosity.

"Well . . . it's not a sin to have sex if you don't pop the girl's cherry."

I don't think I ever asked my friend what his reaction was, as I was laughing so hard that I probably inadvertently hung up on him. The first thing I pictured in my mind was a criminal court trial.

PROSECUTOR: Did you rape my client?

DEFENDANT: I did no such thing!

PROSECUTOR: Do you admit to forcibly putting your penis inside of her?

DEFENDANT: Yes, I do.

PROSECUTOR: Then, how on earth do you expect the people on this jury and the people in this courtroom to believe that you didn't rape my client?

DEFENDANT: BECAUSE I DIDN'T POP HER CHERRY!

I don't remember reading "Thou shall not pop thy neighbor's cherry." However, I never read The Bible, so that verse could actually be in there somewhere. It's probably John 6:9 or something.

Education is the key. If you want the teen pregnancy rate to go down, educate. Make birth control readily available to all teens. Let them know the possible consequences of their actions. Teach them that their bodies are their own, and that it's perfectly natural for them to explore it. Teach them that love and sex do not go hand in hand, but that it is ideal, and it is what they should try to strive for, just because their lives will probably be better if they don't fuck just any shmoe. Teach them sex etiquette. Teach them how to respect their partners . . .

Oh, shit! Was this chapter supposed to be about why guys suck? For a second, it even looked like it was going to be about sex etiquette. Oh well, I'll just have to save those topics for another book, or maybe my Web site. Sorry about that little tangent. My editor says I'm out of space for this chapter. I guess we'll have to find out why guys suck some other time.

CHAPTER 12

Sexual Injustice

For one of the first jobs I ever had, I worked at the mall in a software store. My boss and I were talking about chicks one day, and he said that women will never understand men because if a woman wants to get laid, she can just go out and do it, while a guy doesn't have that luxury.

He was right, too. I believed it before he even said it because I had seen it through the years, over and over again. Chicks pick who they sleep with. Guys take what they can get.

There are guys who have read my site and think I'm a loser. Those guys apparently have had sex with tons of women and have no problems attracting more. Hell, I even have a friend who has had sex with a lot of chicks. If he is to be believed, he's fucked at least 20 different chicks.

The sad fact is, though, that no matter if he had fucked over 30 chicks, there exist chicks who have had more guys than that. In fact, your average chick has had way, way, WAAAAAAAAAAAAAAAAAAAAAY more sex than your average guy, and goddammit it just ain't right.

Guys, almost every chick you know has fucked more than you. Almost every chick you know has had it in more positions than you ever will. Almost every chick you know has had multiple partners at the same time, multiple inputs, and maybe even animals, just to piss you off. And if you know a chick who hasn't had more sex than you have, just wait a few years. She'll beat ya.

Amy has a former roommate and good friend named Bianca. I've never particularly liked Bianca, as she is basically an immature person. She acts immature, looks much younger than she is, has no intellectual interests, and really doesn't find me funny. Amy says Bianca finds me funny, but I know better. I've never really thought Bianca liked me either.

While I do have a bias towards Bianca, I'm not mean to her, and I don't speak down to her. I will sometimes hang out with Amy and Bianca, and things are fine. I accept that Amy doesn't like all of my friends, and I'm not going to necessarily like all of hers.

As I said, Bianca looks younger than she is. She's 25 years old, and looks maybe 16 or 17. She is thin, average height, has short brown hair, big brown eyes, and B-cup tits. She's a clingy chick, very definitely a time whore. She cries easily, and routinely cries in her job, a job involving children. In short, the girl emanates no sexuality whatsoever. Unless you're a pedophile and you just dig that sort of thing, you're not going to find that Bianca gets your juices flowing.

I admit, not only am I biased, but this is all my opinion. However, guys have a tendency to think somewhat alike when it comes to this sort of thing. A chick doesn't have to be attractive to be sexual. People emanate sexuality. It's kind of a spiritual thing. When I met Amy, I could tell she was in touch with her sexuality. It doesn't matter if a person is ugly, fat, thin, funny, dumb, or smart. A chick can be stacked with double-D tits and a great ass, and she may not be sexual because of the clothing she wears or the way she carries herself. Or she may be a slut because that's what guys always look at.

Whatever the case may be, I can say that Bianca is low on the sexuality radiosity scale, to the average (read: most) guy(s).

One night I was using Amy's AOL account, and Bianca sends me an Instant Message™, thinking that I am Amy. I told her that I wasn't, and because we're over the Internet, was able to get some sex talk going. And what I found out made me sick. While I'd like to reprint the transcript that I have of the IM chat we had, I'm pretty paranoid and fear any legal repercussions. So, let me summarize what I found out:

1. Bianca blew guys in cars in the parking lots around the university. I asked how she planned all that out and she said that it just happened.
2. She let a guy do anal on her.
3. She had a threesome with two guys.
4. She never did any lesbian stuff.

Pretty heavy stuff there, huh? A chick who has the sexuality of the Pope has had a fucking threesome! She's done back door, and sucked guys off in the school parking lot many times. And whether or not she admits it, she's only a few drinks away from being bi-curious.

On the other end of the scale, another of Amy's friends is pretty hot. She has a great body, short blonde hair, blue eyes, B-cup tits, and a meaty ass that guys love. She is a supermegaslut. She'd fuck me if she were drunk enough. She has had sex in public, had a threesome where she got drunk, and ate a chick out while being boned by some lucky guy, cheated on just about every boyfriend she ever had, and in fact, used guys for sex. One of her biggest joys was fucking a guy who was genuinely interested in her and then dumping him soon thereafter.

So, the point is that supermegaslutty chicks get hot, kinky sex. Sexuality-less chicks get kinky sex, although I can't be sure if it's hot. And guys? We're damn lucky to get a girl to consider swallowing, much less a threesome.

I've gotten so many emails from chicks saying, "If you just want to get laid, why not go out and do it," like it's as easy as going to the grocery store or something. Maybe I could just go out and get laid, but I'm guessing it'd be more like go out, spend some money on a chick's drinks, don't get laid, move to another chick, buy her some drinks, don't get laid, move to another chick, buy her some drinks, get her wasted, get laid, and get chlamydia while getting her pregnant.

After many months thinking about this, my conclusion is that 80 percent of the chicks are fucking 25 percent of the guys. Think about it. For a chick like Bianca to have a threesome and suck dick in cars, she has to come into contact with many different guys, who are getting other girls to give them threesomes and suck them off in cars. In fact, Bianca's "boyfriend" during this time was a guy who didn't like her at all, but wouldn't turn down the free sex if one of his other bitches couldn't come over that night. I also know that she gave him anal that one time to try to win him back. Meanwhile, he's fucking at least two other chicks.

One night, when Amy lived at the dorms, she and two other chicks were bored. We snuck some drinks into one of the girl's rooms and were trying to figure out something to do.

"Let's play some strip poker," I jokingly suggested.

"That's a great idea!" replied one of Amy's friends. "Do you have any cards?"

"Yes," Amy's other friend said. "Let's play."

"HOLY SHIT!" I thought. "This can't be happening! They've got to be kidding."

They weren't.

What then happened was one of the coolest moments of not only my five-year college career, but indeed my whole life. I played strip poker with three other girls. I got them all out of their tops and down to their panties. They got me down to my boxers, and eventually, out of them. They couldn't believe that I actually took my boxers off.

That meant I was out of the game. They finished playing but didn't take off their panties, and of course I complained about that. What I was hoping was to get a foursome going, but alas, guys can't be in the female dorms past midnight on a weeknight, and it was 11:45pm. I was out of luck, even if I had tried to initiate something.

A few months later, I asked one of those two chicks if she'd give me a threesome with Amy. She told me that she had a boyfriend (whom she had cheated on before, and of course, he had cheated on her before). My response was, "So? This doesn't involve him." She still said no. I had missed the opportunity.

In my chat with Bianca she said that she gave blowjobs in the school parking lot, and that it "just happened." The fact is that Bianca had a roommate who was using the room during the day, and wanted to blow guys who lived at home with their mommies and daddies, but since they still lived with their parents, she could not easily blow them in their homes. So, she, with multiple guys on multiple occasions, "just happened" to blow them in the parking lot while class was in session.

Well, why would a chick play strip poker with me and not fuck me? I mean, shit, I've already seen her practically nude (her underwear was sort of see-through) and she's seen me and I don't have any weird scars or anything. I have no doubt that in her mind, we "just happened" to play strip poker one night. Maybe if I could have planned a way to get her drunk with Amy hanging around, a threesome might have "just happened."

I've had three sexual partners. Amy has had more partners than me. Amy's sisters have had more partners than me. My sister has had more partners than me. My mom has probably had more partners than me. I would say 95 percent of chicks my age have had more partners than me.

While quantity is not quality, all this lack of sex has affected my self-esteem. My sister was fucking before I was, and I knew it. Everyone seemed to be fucking before me. There had to be something wrong with me, because I was missing out. And unlike drugs, fucking was something that I wanted to do.

I have had three sexual partners to date, and Amy is included in that number. The other two sexual partners didn't give me good sex. However, if I were a chick, I could just go out and try again if I didn't get good sex one night.

Many chicks want to be tied up. Many chicks want rough sex. Many chicks even have rape fantasies. However, some don't know that's what they want, and others know it, but are maybe ashamed to tell their partners. So, they go out and find someone to whom they aren't really attached to give them these things. Maybe Guy B will do something Guy A won't.

The same doesn't work for most guys. Most guys want threesomes. Some guys may want to dress up in women's underwear while being fucked in the ass by a chick wearing a dildo. Well, it's going to be damn hard for a guy to find a chick openly willing to do either of those two things.

By and far, chicks control who gets sex, when they get it, and what type of sex they get. Period. It's not only unfair, but it's responsible for many communication problems between men and women. That's why there are guys who believe a chick wants it when she really doesn't. There are chicks who like to say no to guys when they really do mean yes. Women control sex, and guys, like women, want to have sex, so guys will jump through enormous hoops to get some, whether it be dating a chick for a few months even though he really doesn't like her, or spending $500 for an hour of her time in a bordello. Chicks will never understand why guys like me hate and despise them. Eighty percent of chicks are fucking 25 percent of the guys.

I like to do more than bitch. I like to offer solutions as well. My solution would involve all men calling the shots, not allowing chicks to seduce them. This is impossible and will always be, as long as marriage and exclusive relationships exist. Men would have to choose the chicks they fuck, so chicks can see what it's like to have to be smart and make a lot of money and then still be turned down by almost every guy they ask out. Maybe then they can find out about the depression that complete and utter loneliness brings.

Or, perhaps the real solution would be for both sexes to be more open and honest about sex, creating a society of more sexual acceptance than we've ever had before, which would also lead to increased cultural and intellectual tolerance.

Nah, men will routinely be turning down women for sex before that ever happens.

CHAPTER 13

Why Guys Cheat

I recently got an email from a female reader of my site:

Hey wasssup? Just wanted you to know that most of your advice is totally awesome and accurate. There is one thing that I'm dyin to know though, why the hell do guys cheat on their girlfriends??? Is there a way that chicks can keep their guys' eyes on them and only them? Please let me know.

Out of the hundreds of thousands of emails I've received, no one has ever asked me that question. However, that question is one that is at the core of relations between the sexes, so I figured I might as well take a stab at it.

First off, the question has biased wording. "Why the hell do guys cheat on their girlfriends?" As we all know, women cheat too. That question is akin to, "Why do white people smell funny?" As most of us know, not all white people smell funny.

So, if you allow me to take some liberty with the question, I'm actually going to break it up into two: "Why do men have a propensity towards cheating?" and "Why do the men that cheat, cheat?"

Why do men have a propensity towards cheating?

There are lots of theories to this one, and more than likely a combination of them actually holds true. The biggest theory is that the male species has it in their genetic code to spread their seed. Monogamy is unnatural in the Animal Kingdom, and since human beings are part of that group, we males are major sluts. Along the same lines, other theories suggest that having multiple partners is a way to increase territory as well.

This may have something to do with why men are predisposed to cheating. Nature works in mysterious ways sometimes. Studies have shown that women are more likely to cheat when they are menstruating than at any other time on their cycle. Nature has a lot to do with the answer to this question.

But, as with everything in life, it's a little more complicated than that. I buy the whole nature argument, but I also believe that there are a lot of cultural reasons guys cheat as well. Guys brag about how many partners they have. Money equals power, and that equals women. And while this is debatable, I do believe that most men are unhappier than most women. It's why we die younger than chicks.

Lack of happiness plays a huge role in cheating. Lack of fulfillment is the number one reason women cheat on their men. I believe many men can have fulfilling relationships, yet still cheat, because they always want more. However, lack of fulfillment is a huge reason why both sexes cheat. So women, if your guy is happy, he may cheat. If he's not happy, he's much more likely to cheat.

Why do the men that cheat, cheat?

I do not think that the above theories on nature answer this question very well. It's a natural urge to eat all we can get in our mouths. It's a natural urge to beat stupid people senseless, yet many people can easily control their appetites and their temper. Sexual urges may be the strongest of all, yet most people are not really so weak that they have no control over them.

I'm sorry if I sound like a broken CD (vinyl records are soooo 1963), but the true reason that men cheat, at least in today's society, is that men are simply the beggars, not the choosers. When it comes to fucking, men have to take what they can get. It is not every day that the average guy gets offered sex. In our society, it is the men that must court the women. In cases where women show interest in a guy, the poor shmuck probably has never experienced that before, or at the most, very rarely. If there were ever any girls interested in me, I still do not know about them.

Have you ever seen a guy smitten by a beautiful woman? It's hysterical. We turn into little schoolgirls. Oh, I've done it. I've seen other guys do it as well. Just talking to a beautiful woman enhances our self-esteem. Just watch a normal guy having a conversation with a fine lass for the first time. You'll notice him blushing and trying to hide his smile.

I have a great story that illustrates this point. I had gone out to Los Angeles for a trip and went to an acquaintance's house. We talked for a little bit and he was telling me that his next-door neighbor was this hot actress and that I'd have to meet her. She eventually came home and my acquaintance invited her over. I asked her what she had acted in and she said she did an episode of *The Sopranos*. I was immediately impressed. I asked if she had a tape of it and she did. She went to her place and got it and came back and showed us her work on *The Sopranos*.

I never watched *The Sopranos* before. It was still amazing to see this chick in a bit part, though. She had a few lines and I thought that she was the best actress ever because I was so smitten with her. She really was nice and we got along great. I should have scored her digits.

So, I purchased *The Sopranos* DVD sets for Amy this past Christmas. I had never watched the show before and never wanted to start watching it because I didn't know the whole story. I would only watch the show from the beginning and I knew Amy had wanted to see it.

While I'm enjoying almost every episode we watch, I'm constantly waiting for the scene that this chick was in. I told Amy that I met one of the extras. Finally, near the end of season two, her scene comes on, AND IT'S THE WORST ACTING I'VE EVER SEEN ON *THE SOPRANOS*.

In fact, the acting was so bad that later on in the episode, one of the characters asks about the actress' character. The response was, "She just never came by again." I think the producers took her off the show because she couldn't act.

The Sopranos is one of the best-acted and casted shows ever. She was horrible. But when she was in front of me, she was awesome and I loved her and thought she should get an Oscar.

My point is that guys are stereotyped as being cheaters and users, yet when you see them blushing and drooling over a beautiful girl, it's just hard to accept that most guys are assholes.

The guys that do approach beautiful women are usually good-looking assholes. They're called assholes either because all other men envy them, or because they're actually assholes. When a woman approaches us, though, it takes us completely by surprise, every time. Women control who gets the pussy. Guys can only hope they'll be among the chosen.

"But wait a second, CSG," you think. "What if a guy is in a happy, committed relationship? Why would he even risk throwing that all away?"

When we're smitten, we're not thinking of our wives/girlfriends, or our kids. We're thinking of nookie. We're also thinking, "Holy shit! I can't believe I'm going to get some nookie!" Believe me, there's nothing in the world like strange poon.

As I said above, the deck is stacked against us from the start. When we're married, it's even tougher, as women seem to flock to married guys. I went to a friend's bachelor party. We were standing outside of a bar, in the parking lot actually, trying to figure out what we were going to do next.

All of a sudden, these two hot chicks walk by and ask us if we have the time. We tell them what time it is and they thank us and walk inside. We stare at them the entire time. Finally, one of us says, "I bet they'd go out with me."

"No way they'd go out with you, they want me."

One guy says, "Actually, out of all the guys here, if they were to pick one of us, they would pick me, and that's a fact."

He said it so definitively, I thought, "Man, what a prick."

"You know why they would pick me over each and every one of you?" he asks.

Nobody answers.

"Here's why." He lifts up his left hand, and his ring finger has a wedding band. "When you're married, you get approached much more than when you're single."

So, what's a girl to do? While it may sound radical, having a relationship based around honesty and communication is the key. Also, realize that no one is perfect by any means. In fact, if you expect a guy to cheat on you, then it's going to be a lot less painful when he actually does.

If your partner and you are mature enough to handle it, try spicing up your sex life with more creative ideas and maybe involve other people. I have had sex with other chicks since I've been with Amy and I do not consider it cheating because she knows about each one.

Guys, if you establish an open line of communication in your relationship, then you may be able to discuss your feelings with your partner before you cheat. Whether it's, "You're not satisfying me recently," or, "There's this hot new intern at work who really turns me on," chances are that if you communicate and your relationship is mature enough that you won't cheat and ruin your own relationship.

I'm lucky with Amy. She realizes that there is a difference between sex and love, and she also realizes that I have had fewer partners than she has. She didn't particularly like the fact that I fucked some bitch, but she understands why I did it, and the fact that I'm with her and not that bitch means something.

If you know that your partner could never ever handle finding out about your cheating, than either don't cheat at all, or don't get caught.

In most cases, cheating is not a big deal. Women, you should not freak out if you find out your man is cheating. What you should do is let your partner know how deeply hurt and disappointed you are. Yelling at him will only reinforce why he cheated on you to begin with. Think about whether or not your relationship is salvageable logically and calmly. Cool off for a few days. From there, make a decision. However, if he's fucking a relative or a close friend, don't give him a second chance.

CHAPTER 14

Amy Fisher Is Normal

I was flicking through my TV's channels last weekend when I saw MSNBC was doing a piece on Amy Fisher, the so-called Long Island Lolita.

For my non-U.S. readers, let me jog your memory. Amy Fisher says she was dating an older married man by the name of Joey Buttafuoco. She wanted to be with him forever, so she shot his wife, Mary Jo, in the face at point-blank range. Ah, the things that love causes young people to do.

She did not kill Mary Jo, and Amy Fisher was tried and convicted of attempted murder. That was in 1992.

Amy Fisher is now out of prison, and everyone involved seems to have put the incident behind them. Fisher has publicly apologized to Mary Jo, and Joey and Mary Jo are no longer married. Amy's biggest question after getting out of prison was, "Now what?" What could she do, now that she is out of prison?

Why, go to college of course! Oh, and she's dating a 51-year-old too. She's 24 years old and she's dating someone over twice her age!

An aberration? I mean, after all, I'm talking about a girl who shot someone point-blank in the face. Why, of course not.

Jenny McCarthy, Shoshanna Lonstein, Anna Nicole Smith, Annette Benning, Catherine Zeta Jones, to name a few.

But these are celebrities! Sorry to inform you, but Hollywood's dysfunctions are just a reflection of our own.

I am not going to fault an older guy for wanting to be with young girls. There's nothing wrong with that. Women get face lifts, tummy tucks, and liposuction to feel younger. Guys just find a young, willing hottie. That, I understand.

However, I do not understand what these girls, many of them attractive, and a few of them even smart, see in someone who is going to be on Medicare in just two decades.

They'd probably say that these guys are more mature than guys their age. Fuck that and fuck you! I've always been mature for my age. Always. Have younger girls ever thrown themselves at me? NO. Hell, older girls have never thrown themselves at me either.

It isn't even a money thing. That makes it even more perplexing. When I was in college, I was interested in a girl who seemed to like me. I asked her out. She turned me down. She wanted to be sure that my feelings weren't hurt, though. She told me she did like me as a friend, and she thought I was funny.

A few months later I found out she was dating a 31-year-old who didn't even own a fucking car. She also did his laundry. Now, if this guy didn't own a car, what are the chances that he owned a washer and dryer? She drove him wherever he needed to go, even though she was in school and he, well, I don't know what he did.

When I found out whom she was dating, I was not only hurt, but also appalled and incensed. Here is a girl who wasn't dating anybody. I asked her out. She said no, and a few months later decides to date a pure loser. We don't live in New York City, people. We live in an area of the country where having a car at 30 years old isn't a status symbol, it's a necessity. I had a fucking car, not to mention brains, a sense of humor, and a future that did not involve finding a college girl to do my laundry and drive me places.

I had been rejected a lot of times. I was already bitter. I had respect for this girl, though, because she was straight with me. She didn't play around with my emotions. However, once I found out that she was dating a 31-year-old, I decided that she was going to get lectured by me. I waited to see her and never did. I always kept missing her. So, I sent her an email. I wish I still had it. I basically said, "How DARE you turn me down for a date and then start a relationship with a 31-year-old loser? I guess if that's what you were looking for in a guy I would have sold my car and had you do my laundry."

She wrote me back and basically told me that she did not have to defend her dating life. She could date whomever she chose and it was none of my business. (She was right, by the way.) She even had a friend of hers write to me to ask me to leave her alone, which I did, although I would have left her alone if she had asked me herself.

She eventually broke up with the guy, and apparently came onto one of my former friends (and he apparently turned her down). I eventually did see her on campus and every time I saw her we would talk. She never brought up my tirade, and neither did I. She did lose my respect and my interest. I guess I only talked to her out of kindness, and besides, ignoring her would not have accomplished anything.

I cannot imagine wanting to be with a woman older than my mother. I cannot imagine wanting to be with a woman approaching my mother's age. Yet for many chicks, dating guys who have to take Viagra is apparently the thing to do.

Young women have been dating older men for centuries, but the trend has reached an alarming high within the past few years. What do girls see in Joey Buttafuoco? Is it just a phase?

The saddest thing is that for every girl dating a senior citizen, there is a guy her age that would love to take her out. I see it way too often. Every chick I've ever known that has dated someone twice her age or above could easily get a date from a deserving guy born within the same decade as themselves.

Even my sister won't date a guy close to her age. When she was 14, she was dating a 21-year-old. When she was 17, she started a relationship with a 32-year-old! When my sister dumped the 32-year-old for a guy who was only a few years older than she was, the guy dumped her after three months and my sister had learned her lesson: Don't date guys her own age, as she will get used if she does. She started dating 32-year-old (now 36 or something) again a few weeks later.

But this 32-year-old loves her. And uses her babysitting money when he's short on cash. And, of course, she brings him leftovers from my parent's house when they're done eating, because he doesn't have enough money for food. Oh, and she's not allowed to touch him in public, although he will hug other girls right in front of her, in public.

I tried and tried and tried to tell her she was being a moron. I made fun of her at every opportunity. Her friends would call and I would answer the phone. They'd ask for her and I'd say, "She can't come to the phone right now. She's helping an old man cross the street." I'd ask my sister how they met. "Did he pull up beside you after school and offer you a Snickers bar?" I'd see 90-year-old guys in the grocery store and say, "Hey sister, I think he's single! I'll ask him out for you if you want."

That only made my sister resent me and now she won't tell me anything about their relationship at all. It's too bad, because I know my sister really well. She once met a guy off of the Internet and told me. This was like the first time she met the guy, too. I asked her, "So, did you jack him off?"

"No."

"C'mon, tell me. I know you jacked him off."

"I did not."

"Stop lying to me. I can tell. You jacked him off. Admit it."

"I did not jack him off."

"Ok. I know you jacked him off though."

"Fine! I jacked him off!"

"Are you being serious?" I asked.

"Yes. I am serious. He came over today and I jacked him off. How did you know?"

"I could just tell. Slut."

I somehow knew that she had jacked the guy off. It pains me to see my sister wasting her years with this older loser, and she won't talk to me about him at all, when I could truly help.

My sister suffers from Clingy Chick Syndrome, or CCS. Basically, CCS is when a chick would rather be with someone (that is, have a boyfriend) than be alone (that is, not have a boyfriend). Being in an unhappy relationship is better than not having a relationship at all. That's why she went back to 32-year-old as soon as she could. Before she dated the guy closer to her age, she pressed the 32-year-old for a strong commitment. He said no. My sister started dating someone else. As soon as she got dumped, she went right back to him.

Does CCS affect someone you know? Probably so. Unfortunately, there is no cure for CCS, other than letting it run its course. Ancient doctors thought that a couple of good smacks in the head would do the trick, but it never has.

If my sister did not have CCS, she'd be a happier person. So would all the girls who have CCS. Instead of going back to 32-year-old, she would have maybe analyzed why she got dumped and realized that she was either getting played from the beginning or that she was too clingy. If she had been by herself and truly thought things through, she would have realized that she was unhappy with 32-year-old and would have tried to avoid some of the pitfalls she had just been through and apply that to her next relationship.

That's scary, though. It can be hard to get yourself to admit that you did some things wrong and that the past few years of your life were for naught. If you go back to 32-year-old, you at least know what you're getting, which is better than being single, right?

The reason that I say it's acceptable for older men to want to date younger women is because the older guys know exactly what they want. Usually, a trophy. Having a young girl is like having bragging rights. It makes you feel younger. The reason I'm against younger women actually dating older guys is because the guys wind up using them, and they don't actually care about them in most cases. And it's not like there aren't guys their own ages that won't go out with them. These girls won't even give guys their own age a chance.

While my sister has yet to shoot anyone in the face, she, and millions of girls like her are basically just like Amy Fisher without a gun. I can guarantee you that if things don't work out between Amy Fisher and her current arthritis-suffering boyfriend, she'll bounce right back and date someone else just as old or older.

At least Amy Fisher had seven years to think about it, which is much more than most girls her age have ever had. But if she had seven years and still hasn't made the right choice, then most girls probably wouldn't make the right choice either.

It seems like I'll just have to wait until I'm 46 years old to date girls in their 20s. I guess I'll start reading *War and Peace* now.

CHAPTER 15

Revelations

I have an irrational fear of cockroaches. Ever since I was a kid, I've been terrified of them.

In one of my earliest childhood memories, I'm four or five years old, and my mom is cooking breakfast and my dad is getting dressed in their bedroom. I'm in the living room and I see a cockroach and I run down the hall into my dad's room and jump on his bed, just to get away from it.

To this day, I am still afraid of cockroaches. I used to be afraid of spiders too, and probably would still be if I saw a really huge one. However, regular spiders don't scare me anymore. Cockroaches still do.

That's one thing that sucks about living alone. If there's a cockroach in the bathroom, it becomes a huge ordeal. One morning I woke up, walked into the bathroom, and took a shit. When I sit on the john at my apartment, I usually take off my pants and underwear completely. *(Note: I do not do this on the rare occasions when I have to number two in public.)* This morning was no exception. I threw my boxers down in front of my feet. I finished my business, wiped up a bit and went to put on my boxers and a humongous cockroach comes running from underneath them!

I was TERRIFIED. I ran into my bedroom and let out a weird scream, one of disgust. I eventually went back into the bathroom and saw that the roach had gone into the bathtub. What a lucky break. I turned on the shower and the cockroach was never seen by me again.

One time, Amy was down here visiting and as I went into my bedroom to get ready for bed, a huge cockroach was on my nightstand, right next to where I sleep.[8] I told Amy and she went in and killed it for me. Had she not done that, I would have been sleeping on the couch, hoping the cockroach would just not be there the next day.

There's something that scares guys kind of the way cockroaches scare me, and that's commitment. And ladies, it's not just in relationships. I waited literally as long as I could before committing myself to college. I knew I was going to go to college, but I did not know which one, and making that decision was terrifying, as I felt like I was going to be locked into it for four or more years. I am sure many guys and girls went through a bit of angst choosing a college as well.

However, women as a whole[9] are much less afraid of commitment. In fact, after you date the same girl for a few weeks, they're already practically asking you when you're going to marry them.

I wrote on my Web site that anyone who gets married before the age of 25 is an idiot. I should change that. It should read, "Anyone except me who gets married before the age of 25 is an idiot."

Yes, I'm getting married. I'll be 24 in just a few months.

Now I have to defend myself a bit. First, I am not 19 years old. I am a college graduate who has moved from the city in which he went to college and now lives alone. I have no friends here. When I am here on the weekends, either a friend of mine comes to visit me or I run some errands or just don't do anything at all. My life is completely boring and miserable and the only reason I put up with it is because my salary is quite good.

Why don't I update my Web site? Because I do not have a high-speed Internet connection and I have no stories to tell anyway. I don't fucking do anything.

I've been dating Amy for three years, which of course is no time at all compared to a long marriage. However, getting married to her just makes sense to me. I work as a contractor, for one, and while I am extremely overcompensated for what it is I do, I do not get benefits. If I marry her and she gets a decent job, boom, I get benefits.

---

[8] And no, I do not live in an infested apartment in the ghetto. I live in nice apartments surrounded by a lake and tons of trees, hence the insects.

[9] No pun intended.

I also do not live in the city where I graduated college. I live a few hours away. It just makes sense that if she's going to come down here that we're married when she does.

And it's not like the chicks are banging down my front door. And I live in the most boring city on the fucking planet. In fact, if I had known how boring this place was, I would have never moved here. Being well paid does not equate to being happy, although it doesn't hurt. When she moves down here, at least I will have someone to share my misery with.

I've also started looking for work elsewhere and she knows that. Turns out that she could literally move down here after we get married, and then move again somewhere else. I am still in the South and am looking to change that as soon as possible.

I've asked her if anything is going to change in our relationship after we're married and she says no. So far she's been pretty good about things like that. The first time I told her I had sex with someone else, I feared something would change in our relationship. Nothing ever did. If anything, I appreciated her more for giving me that freedom.

If I thought it would change our relationship, I would not marry her. But I still have plenty of fears. Things can still change regardless of what people say. I haven't changed that much since I was 15, however she has changed drastically since she was 15. Will we get sick of each other? Will we drive each other crazy? Will she make me dress up in her underwear and take my picture? Can I possibly persuade her to join the local swinger's club?

By the time you read this I will have married Amy. Maybe I shouldn't be getting married so young, but she is the only person who has ever accepted me for me. I kind of don't like the fact that I'm marrying the first chick I laid, however I have laid others since, so it doesn't bother me too much.

When it all comes down to it, I'm marrying her for good reasons: tax benefits, actual job benefits, someone to always be around me, pussy whenever I want, and, oh yeah . . . I actually love her.

And I'm really fucking scared of cockroaches.

Printed in the United States
4944